# JOAN CRAWFORD

## THE ENDURING STAR

## PETER COWIE

FOREWORD BY MICK LASALLE    AFTERWORD BY GEORGE CUKOR

*RIZZOLI*
NEW YORK

First published in the United States of America in 2009
by Rizzoli International Publications, Inc.
300 Park Avenue South
New York, NY 10010
www.rizzoliusa.com

© 2009 Peter Cowie
Foreword text © Mick LaSalle
Afterword text reprinted courtesy of The Estate of George Cukor

2009 2010 2011 2012 / 10 9 8 7 6 5 4 3 2 1

Distributed in the U.S. trade by Random House, New York
Printed in China

ISBN: 978-0-8478-3066-4
Library of Congress Control Number: 2008933249

PHOTO CREDITS

Cinémathèque Suisse, Lausanne: iv, vii, 5, 6-7, 12, 17, 19, 22, 24, 41, 43,
45, 54, 72, 79, 81, 86, 87, 88, 89, 91, 96, 97 l, 101, 102, 111, 112, 134, 135,
136, 137, 139, 142, 145, 147, 148, 152, 155, 161, 170, 171 l, 172, 173, 177,
183, 184, 185, 186, 189, 192, 194, 195, 197, 198, 199, 200, 201, 202, 203,
204, 210, 211, 212-13, 218, 224.

George Eastman House Motion Picture Department Collection:
x, 14, 18, 21, 40, 59, 67, 83, 100, 149, 153, 166-67, 178, 181, 190.

The Kobal Collection/The Picture Desk/MGM: i, ii, iii, v, vi, xii, 3, 8,
13, 15, 27, 33, 36, 38, 46-47, 48, 53, 56, 58, 60, 61, 63, 64, 65, 66, 70, 71,
73, 74, 75, 76, 77, 80, 84, 93, 98, 99, 104 05, 107, 113, 114, 115, 118-19,
120, 121, 122, 123, 125, 126, 129, 130 31, 132, 140, 141, 143, 144, 150,
151, 154, 156, 157, 158, 162, 164, 165, 171 r, 174, 214-15. The Kobal
Collection/The Picture Desk/Warner Bros.: viii-ix, 168, 176, 179,
188, 207. The Kobal Collection/The Picture Desk: 82 (United Artists);
193 (RKO); 187 (20th Century Fox).

Photofest: 10, 11, 16, 20, 23, 25, 29, 30, 31, 32, 34, 35, 37, 39, 42, 44,
50, 51, 52, 55, 57, 62, 68, 69, 78, 90, 94, 95, 97 r, 103, 108, 109, 110,
116, 117, 127, 138, 159, 160, 175, 182, 191, 196, 205, 206, 209, 216, 226.

~ ABOVE *On the set of* Chained *(1934), with Clark Gable in the background.*

~ PREVIOUS PAGE I *Photo by George Hurrell, 1932.* PAGES II-III *Publicity shots of the late 1920s and early 1930s tended to emphasize Joan's come-hither look. Photo on right by George Hurrell.* PAGE IV *Ca. 1943.* PAGE V *Photo by George Hurrell, 1932.* PAGE VI *Wavy hair made Joan seem softer and more vulnerable.* PAGE VII *Studio portrait for* The Damned Don't Cry *(1950).* TITLE PAGE *Joan Crawford: the most elegant of stars, in* The Damned Don't Cry *(1950).*

# CONTENTS

# FOREWORD

*Mick LaSalle*

TOO OFTEN FILM HISTORY looks through the wrong end of the telescope. Careers have been assessed on the basis of things that came later— the later films, when the star was already fading, or later events. And so there are epic distortions: Marilyn Monroe and James Dean as seen through the prism of early death, John Wayne as interpreted through his politics, and Norma Shearer as transformed into the forgiving milquetoast that she played once and only once in *The Women*.

Contemporaries always know better. If we, for example, were to talk about Julia Roberts, what initially comes to mind is *Pretty Woman*. We'd remember that first clear impression and what it meant to us. But with classic stars, alas, the contemporaries are just about gone, while the distortions and misimpressions surrounding notable careers are close to unkillable. If only we could just get back to that moment, when a big-eyed flapper from Texas connected with the people in the twelfth row, we'd understand everything about Joan Crawford that we need to know.

Joan Crawford. More than a hundred years after her birth, hers is still a name to be reckoned with, a name to say and then pause for a second as the images come flooding in. Yet, for all the power built into the very notion of Crawford, she may be the ultimate victim of that backwards telescope. Today's audiences frequently ignore the younger Crawford and look for signs of the later Crawford (of *Trog* or *Strait-Jacket*) in the performances of her middle years. Likewise, in her most wonderfully bitchy turns, audiences see (or imagine) parallels in Crawford's personal life.

In perceiving Crawford as some grand movie monster, sacred or otherwise, there's undoubtedly a whiff of sadism. Thus, a powerful woman gets her comeuppance. More significant, relegating Crawford to the realm of cliché makes it that much easier for us to ignore the colossal demands she makes on us. Look at her in the pages of this book: She wants approval, our approval. She wants it as much or more than any star ever did. Yet she's not sentimental about it. She knows us. She knows exactly what we're worth, and her directness is a little intimidating.

In a way, Crawford's career is the classic American story with the classic American result. She put value in achievement and searched for

~ OPPOSITE **Sadie McKee** *(1934), costume by Adrian and photo by George Hurrell.*

love, definition, and salvation in the public realm, leaving her personal life to fend for itself. And so she ended up with great fame and success and a personal life that seems, at best, vestigial. Her career's final chapter, in which she'd star in virtually any low-budget atrocity, even if it meant playing horrible caricatures of herself, constitutes a cautionary tale that Americans recoil from because we know it all too well. If you've ever posted a YouTube video of yourself, or commented on a blog, or imagined yourself on a reality TV show, or standing there thanking the Academy—then you know the Crawford impulse. You know that love-me-or-I'll-kill-you hunger.

But Crawford is different from us in that she had more guts. She had more drive. She probably had more talent, even if it seemed she brought her talent into being through sheer force of will. No matter. However she did it, she did it, and her legacy is incandescent, vibrant, one of a kind—and quite possibly eternal.

You can see her special quality in the photos here, the unstoppable velocity of them. They're not mere records of her art but art in themselves. In them, Crawford does something no one else ever tried before. She stares down posterity. She stands in a room in 1932 as if saying, "Yes, I'm going to be dead someday, but guess what, buster? I'm here now, and you're here with me, and when you're gone, I'll still be here, staring down someone else." Truly, no one else took pictures like these. Pictures of Jean Harlow, at the same studio, captured a moment. Pictures of Garbo were attempts at timeless art. But a picture of Crawford was and is an effort at intimate engagement.

She's connecting with somebody. *You*, to be specific. And in that moment of connection, time disappears. Look at that face—modern, arch, knowing, passionate, ready to eat the world. That's still something new, that's *today* looking right at

you. In her implacable strength, Crawford is Angelina Jolie and Demi Moore, and in the forthright shopgirls she brought to life in the 1930s, there are the seeds of every working-class heroine Julia Roberts ever played. Indeed, every generation since has had its Crawfords. She's the mother of them, and she transcends them.

In the following pages, Peter Cowie turns the telescope the proper way and gives us Crawford's career in its true proportions. Due consideration, of course, is given to Crawford's achievements in the 1940s and 1950s, most notably at Warner Bros., where she made some of the best-known films, including *Mildred Pierce* (1945), for which she won the Academy Award. Her best work from this period is undeniable and deserves its place in the Crawford canon and legend.

But Cowie gives greater and proper emphasis to Crawford's MGM years in the late 1920s and 1930s, for the simple reason that those years found her at her zenith—of her beauty, her screen image, her photographic legacy, and her popularity. Certainly, the photos make a better case than I can that this is one of the sexiest women who ever stepped in front of a camera. That's easy to see. But look closer—at the flapper kicking it up in *Our Dancing Daughters* (1928). Go back to the young woman from a nowhere town in *Possessed* (1931), who dreamed of luxury and success as though they were everything worth having. Look at Crawford raising one eyebrow and smiling at her leading man, as she did in so many of her movies—that electric look that said and promised so much.

That Joan Crawford is everywhere in the pages of this book. When you see her, you'll feel, maybe for the thousandth time, maybe for that precious first time, what she meant to the fans who originally discovered her. That should be our goal, to see Joan Crawford fresh, for the work she did. She and we deserve nothing less.

# INTRODUCTION

THE INSPIRATION FOR THIS book stemmed from my research for *Louise Brooks, Lulu Forever* (Rizzoli, 2006). Joan Crawford was often linked with Louise in references to the Jazz Age, the flapper era, the frenzy of the Charleston, and even weekends at Hearst Castle. Yet while Louise treated Hollywood with ill-disguised scorn, Joan Crawford embraced it, and would not rest until she had become its star of stars.

By what name do you call someone, long dead, whom you never met? The more I study the films of Joan Crawford, the clearer a demarcation line appears between the first and second halves of her career. During the exuberance of the early years, you would have addressed her almost instinctively as "Joan." After World War II, and the pivotal film that was *Mildred Pierce* (1945), she could be nothing but "Crawford," even though fans might call her "Joanie," and crew members and technicians would mutter, with respect, "Miss Crawford."

She was not so much a star as a firmament in her own right. Joan Crawford's career spanned five decades. Her first screen appearance was in 1925, and her swan song in 1970. She was not an iconic figure who, like Garbo, seemed to float beyond mere mortals. Nor was she the embodiment of seduction, like a Dietrich or a Harlow. Rather she marched through life at the head of an invisible host, demanding fealty from her fans, who saw in her broad-shouldered, smoldering, often trashy allure a transcendental version of their everyday experience. Her raw ambition and disciplined work ethic made her all the more appealing to her widespread audience, embodying as it did the quintessential American dream of rising through the social strata from rags to riches.

A cascade of letters would reach her home each week. She would reply to every one—70,000 a year, and some 3 million by the end of her life. "During the holiday season, between Thanksgiving and New Year (a mere six-week period), she would personally type, sign and mail 10,000 letters."[1]

Crawford's image was immortalized by some of Hollywood's finest photographers, and by none better than George Hurrell during the years 1930 to 1941. Her eyes gaze out at the camera with fearless aplomb, with just the rare, right space between them, as though for a magic third eye.

Her lips are full and inviting, but her stare brooks no opposition. This is a woman who lived life on her own reckless terms and on nobody else's. Married four times, with husbands as varied as leading men Douglas Fairbanks Jr. and Franchot Tone, and Pepsi-Cola chairman Alfred Steele, she also reveled in affairs with stars like Clark Gable and Yul Brynner. "I brought more men to their knees, or actually ruined them, than any other actress in Hollywood history," she confessed late in life.[2]

Only high tragedy and low comedy eluded her on screen, and one wishes that she could have worked with Ernst Lubitsch as Miriam Hopkins and Claudette Colbert did, to their infinite advantage. Yet in that prolific fifteen-year spell between 1925 and 1940, Joan at MGM created a rich assortment of characters, none of whom seemed entirely straightforward, each with conflicting loyalties and emotions. She could switch from the sneering bitterness of the working gal to the calculating hauteur of a would-be aristocrat. As she confesses at the close of *The Shining Hour* (1938), "I look like a lady—sometimes." Her fans wanted Joan to aspire to sophistication and decorum, yet in their hearts adored the fact that she would remain forever one of them.

World War II intervened at a critical moment in Crawford's existence as a star. Younger talents, hungry for stardom, were being discovered. Once peace had been achieved, Crawford reemerged in *Mildred Pierce*, and from that point on she would be more severe, more judgmental.

In her "women of a certain age" period, Joan would exploit her mature looks and her sexual authority in films such as *Humoresque* (1946), alongside John Garfield, in *Possessed* (1947) with Van Heflin, and with Henry Fonda and Dana Andrews in *Daisy Kenyon* (1947)—all leading men who would succumb to her often voracious charms. She could serve as somber, passionate vic-

tim too, in *Sudden Fear* (1952), across the screen from a dangerous Jack Palance. By 1954, she could slip with energy and élan into her butch role as gun queen of the Arizona frontier in *Johnny Guitar* (1954), grittier than any man and obsessed with her dreams of building a new township.

Crawford's final years in Hollywood saw her become a grotesque parody of herself. As the lonesome older woman grasping at romance in *Autumn Leaves* (1956), as the axe murderess in *Strait-Jacket* (1964), as the lusty circus owner in *Berserk!* (1968), or as the anthropologist in *Trog* (1970), she flung herself head and shoulders into the fray, unable in her late fifties and early sixties to abandon herself to either wit or wisdom. She would give her fans one major, hallucinating performance during this spell, as Blanche Hudson in *What Ever Happened to Baby Jane?* (1962), Robert Aldrich's savage tale of two sisters joined in mutual loathing and despair, struggling for supremacy in a rancid Los Angeles mansion.

Most stars have neither sufficient time nor pretension to contemplate their role in posterity. Joan Crawford's day in her sixties must have seemed to her as busy as her day in the 1920s. However, had she retired from the movies, like Garbo, at the age of thirty-six, her reputation might be greater than it is today. Had she never adopted children, that reputation certainly would be on an altogether loftier plane. Had Joan never become Crawford...

Marlene Dietrich made less than half as many films as Crawford, as did Norma Shearer. Garbo appeared in only twenty-five features in Hollywood. And while Joan's archrival, Bette Davis, matched her in terms of output, she achieved enduring fame only in her thirties. Joan was never the critics' darling. Across the years she received a mere three Oscar nominations as Best Actress, winning just once (for *Mildred Pierce*). By

comparison, Davis earned eleven nominations, winning twice. Joan's was not such a meager haul, however. Even MGM's favorite, Norma Shearer, took home the Academy Award but once. Garbo received four nominations as Best Actress, but won none. Dietrich was nominated for Best Actress on only one occasion (for *Morocco*).

Anyone younger than forty years of age seems to assume that Crawford was a tasteless monster who mistreated her children, and whose screen presence consists of a prison matron's hairdo, a gigantic mouth made more predatory by lip gloss, and a loathing for men and women alike.

Posthumously condemned as an appalling parent, Crawford has suffered two further accusations, repeated like mantras by successive biographers and journalists: that she had limited skills as an actress and that she never possessed authentic sexual appeal. The testimony of Cathy Crawford Lalande, the daughter Joan adopted in 1947 with her twin sister Cindy, has redressed the balance. "I wouldn't have chosen any other mother in the whole world," she told Charlotte Chandler, "because I had the best one anyone could ever have."[3]

The riposte to all this lies in the heritage of her filmography—in the dozens of films she made in the 1920s, 1930s, and 1940s, with their vast range of personality and emotions. As the photographs in this book attest, Joan exuded a carnal magnetism and a radiant lust for life. Stardom was her lodestone, and she achieved it through a single-minded concentration on crafting her image, cultivating her fan base, and working with individuals like costume designer Adrian and portraitist Hurrell to establish herself as a fashion icon. Although her successive marriages also may have helped keep her in the public eye, I find her private life essentially unexciting compared to her "life," or rather "lives," on screen. Occasionally, as in the early films with Clark Gable, some knowledge of her passions may be instructive, but when all the gossip has died down, when all the yellow press has crumbled into dust, Joan Crawford's screen charisma will ensure her place among the very finest stars produced by Hollywood.

ONE

——

# A TALENT FOR LIVING

(1904 TO 1929)

*"Everything for her is acting; this is her life, her food, her drink."*

JEAN NEGULESCO

T HE LIFE AND CAREER OF Joan Crawford were marked indelibly by the two great wars of her century. When she came to Hollywood in the mid-1920s, the situation of women had changed dramatically in the wake of World War I—in terms of dress, fashion, and moral comportment—on and off the screen. These were the heady days of pre-censorship Hollywood before the imposition of the Production Code. Hollywood throbbed with scandal, from the murder of director William Desmond Taylor in 1922 to the mysterious death of Thomas Ince aboard William Randolph Hearst's yacht in 1924 (evoked by Peter Bogdanovich in his 2001 film, *The Cat's Meow*). Theda Bara, who had embodied the Vamp, had been succeeded by Gloria Swanson, whose risqué roles were caught, in the words of Mick LaSalle, "between Victorian purity and modern openness.... She was assumed to be loose, but in fact she was innocent."[2] On the big screen, costumes had become more revealing by the month. Off screen, nude photographs of stars and starlets, from Ramon Novarro to Louise Brooks, were freely available. Such was the bawdy universe in which Joan Crawford's star could wax and shine.

On March 23, 1908, by her own reckoning (although the real date may have been 1905, or even 1904), Lucille Fay LeSueur was born San Antonio, Texas, of a Swedish-Irish mother and a French-Canadian father. She endured an impoverished childhood. The father left home soon after the birth of his daughter, the mother moved to Lawton, Oklahoma, and Thomas Cassin, Lucille's stepfather, also departed after some years, leaving the young girl grief-stricken. "'Daddy' Cassin was the eternal optimist," she recalled subsequently.[3]

~ OPPOSITE  *Milliners everywhere would owe a great deal to Joan's fondness for hats. Photo by Ruth Harriet Louise, 1925.*

~ PREVIOUS  *The ambitious young Lucille LeSueur, on the verge of being launched as "Joan Crawford."*

Joan, or Billie as she was then known, was sent to one brutal school after another. The fact that she was beaten and punished so cruelly bred in her a fierce independence, an obsession with cleanliness and order, with obedience and perseverance. She did, however, find time for dancing and performing. With her petite stature, her lustrous, dark brown hair, and her freckled features, Joan in her late teens decided to seek her fortune away from her feckless mother and yet another "stepfather," Harry Hough. She seems to have done everything within and beyond reason, posing nude for peep-show vignettes, stripping in Chicago, dancing in Detroit, and then having the luck to be spotted by the legendary J. J. Shubert, who offered her a job in the chorus line of his New York show *Innocent Eyes*, alongside the legendary Mistinguett.

Joan blossomed in Manhattan during the early 1920s, dating men right, left, and center, and honing her hoofing skills in Harlem nightclubs until she had acquired more than a hundred trophies for dancing the Charleston in exhibition contests.[4] Like her contemporary Louise Brooks, she thrived on the generosity of adoring males. "The men we dated," she said, "expected to spend money on us, and usually there was no bad scene if we didn't live up to their—er, sexual expectations. Candy, flowers, great dinners, even furs—we got 'em all."[5] As in her film *Our Blushing Brides* (1930), she shared a room with four friends on 50th Street just off Fifth Avenue. "Our beds stood in a row like the dwarfs' in *Snow White*. You could tell which corner was mine—the window was plastered with my hankies, panties and stockings (I had two pairs). When it was cold enough, they froze."[6]

∽ OPPOSITE  *MGM studio portrait, ca. 1926.*

∽ BELOW  *With cameraman John Arnold, showing a little-known Joan the new 10-kilowatt incandescent globes being introduced on MGM sets, 1928.*

A talent scout from MGM, Harry Rapf, spotted her on stage, arranged screen tests, and persuaded the studio to give her a five-year contract (subject to a six-month probationary period) at $75 a week. On New Year's Day 1925, at the age of twenty-one (or nineteen, according to Joan), she took the train to the Coast—an exhausting two-day journey, as she had spent the studio's travel allowance on Christmas gifts for friends and a selection of clothes and accessories for herself.

## A DESIRE TO DO HER BEST

*"Crawford at this period had an irresistible vivacity, and already much of that compelling quality of personality that transcended questions of mere talent to make her a great star of three succeeding decades."*

—DAVID ROBINSON, *HOLLYWOOD IN THE TWENTIES*[7]

Frederica Sagor Maas, a screenwriter at MGM, described Joan soon after her arrival at the studio in terms that might be applied to Sadie Thompson in *Rain*: "She was a gum-chewing dame, heavily made up...wildly frizzed hair. An obvious strumpet. Crude as she was, everything about her seemed to say, 'Look out. I'm in a hurry. Make room.'"[8]

Joan, with no formal qualifications to her name or any training as an actress, was pitched into no fewer than nine films during 1925, her first

full year at Metro. She was sometimes an extra, sometimes she had a bit part, and in Frank Borzage's *The Circle* (1925) she was the beauty running off with her lover in the prologue. "Due to an error," notes historian Hervé Dumont, "her involvement in the film was never mentioned; [Harry] Rapf was her 'protector.'"[9] Joan kept in the public eye, dating attractive men (providing they could dance well), and accepting whatever the studio offered her, which included serving as Norma Shearer's double in *Lady of the Night* (1925). In the words of F. Scott Fitzgerald, she was "doubt-less the best example of the flapper, the girl you see at smart night clubs, gowned to the apex of sophistication, toying iced glasses with a remote, faintly bitter expression, dancing deliciously, laughing a great deal, with wide, hurt eyes. Young things with a talent for living."[10] Joan mutated

from Lucille LeSueur to Joan Crawford in August 1925, after the studio had organized a contest in *Movie Weekly* magazine, asking for a name that would suit her personality, sound "euphonious," and be "simple to pronounce."

The ubiquitous Joan even appeared as an extra in Erich von Stroheim's ill-fated *The Merry Widow* (1925), and in *Sally, Irene and Mary* (1925), directed by Edmund Goulding, she perished in a train wreck with the man who has loved her from the outset. Many years later, Joan would tell Jack Warner that "Joan Crawford never dies in her films," but in her first season at Metro she could hardly quibble about such a dramatic finale.

Quick-witted, and assimilating advice from experienced talents like cameraman John Arnold, director Eddie Goulding, actress Eleanor Board-man, and actor John Gilbert (who told her to keep

~ OPPOSITE *Joan in* The Boob *(1926).*

~ ABOVE *With Harry Langdon in* Tramp, Tramp, Tramp *(1926).*

her "vitality undiluted on the screen, never to let down for a moment"[11]). Joan was nominated "Miss MGM" for 1925, and the next year an association of some hundred key publicists hailed her as one of the girls most likely to achieve stardom (her fellow nominees included Fay Wray, Dolores Costello, Mary Astor, Janet Gaynor, and Dolores Del Rio).[12] By day, she would learn the names of every crew member on the set. By night, in her bungalow on North Roxbury Drive in Beverly Hills, she wrote personally to thank the hundreds of fans who had sent her letters. Already Joan appreciated that the role of her audience would be as important to her career as the roles she herself inhabited. Responding to their letters was only one aspect of her commitment. She also learned to smile constantly in public, to attend all the right premieres, and to be immaculately groomed for every public occasion.

Harry Langdon selected Joan to be his love interest in *Tramp, Tramp, Tramp* (1926) where she was coy and proper, the daughter of a shoe magnate. In *The Boob* (1926), under the direction of William Wellman, she played "one of Uncle Sam's crack revenue agents," on the track of bootleggers. Her hair was waved and cut short at the neck. Her mouth was still a cupid's bow. But Joan exerted a distinct authority in her scenes, holding herself confidently and glaring at those who would intimidate her.

The following year brought her a charismatic part as a gypsy opposite Lon Chaney, in *The Unknown* (1927). Directed by Tod Browning, this subversive movie about jealousy in a circus milieu boasted delicate, almost surreal sets by Cedric Gibbons. A sloe-eyed Joan could strut and stretch in shorts and a halter in those pre-Code days, unmindfully driving Chaney's "Alonzo the

~ OPPOSITE *Joan in* The Unknown *(1927). Lon Chaney is off screen tossing the knives with his feet.*

~ ABOVE *Joan practicing some dance steps with Ramon Novarro in* Across to Singapore *(1928).*

Armless" to infatuation and murder. Chaney, she observed, "demanded so much from me I was scared, but I seemed to do it right."[13] In *Across to Singapore* (1928), her range and confidence increased. Playing opposite Ramon Novarro, she promised much with her fresh, open smile, her wide, guileless gaze, and her hair—curly, fair, and wavy, even braided at one point. She could exhibit tenderness, and she could conceal her anguish and confusion beneath a pert appearance. Joan made the transition from silence to sound more smoothly than many stars (including poor John Gilbert, with whom Joan shared an onscreen chemistry and complicity in *Twelve Miles Out* [1927] and *Four Walls* [1928]). MGM studio head Louis B. Mayer was so pleased with her progress that he instructed the script department to write a juicy part for her in *Our Dancing Daughters* (1928).

On New Year's Eve 1927, Joan received her first proposal of marriage. The suitor was Douglas Fairbanks Jr., son of Hollywood's most charismatic star, who himself was married to Mary Pickford, the town's favorite sweetheart. "Dodo," or "Doubles," as Joan called her fiancé, had sleek brown hair, a slender face and slim figure, with even finer features than his athletic father. Reared like royalty in his parents' domain at Pickfair on Summit Drive in the San Ysidro Canyon, Douglas Jr. introduced Joan to a cultivated world. She swiftly learned how to arrange a dinner party, how to dress elegantly for different social occasions, and how to behave when meeting luminaries such as Lord and Lady Mountbatten or Noël Coward. He persuaded her to tackle writers like Shaw, Ibsen, or Edna St. Vincent Millay. In later years, when asked to reflect on the ultimate failure of

~ OPPOSITE *MGM promoted the romantic liaison with Douglas Fairbanks Jr.*

~ ABOVE Our Dancing Daughters *(1928).*

their marriage, Fairbanks responded astutely that Joan "was a very sweet girl, but she was also uncultured and uneducated, except in life, which I certainly was not."[14] They would marry on June 3, 1929, in New York City, accompanied by a handful of friends and Fairbanks's mother, Beth.

*Our Dancing Daughters* became a box-office hit, the first of Joan's films to gross more than $1 million. As Joan remembered, "Everything about this picture was inspired. I'd never seen such clothes. I'd never seen such sets as those Cedric Gibbons created. Our location at Carmel was idyllic."[15] Joan would later reiterate like a mantra her complaint that Metro obliged her to do dancing roles. "I had to fight terribly for good parts, because they thought of me as a dancer, and I wanted to get out of those dancing roles."[16] But her twinkle-toed skills were in tune with the times. *Our Dancing Daughters* defined an era. It also

defined Joan's ambition: "You want to take all of life, don't you?" asks her boyfriend, and she responds, "Yes—all. I want to hold out my hands and catch it—like the sunlight." She reveled in the naughtiness of pre-Code Hollywood, abandoning her skirt and flashing her legs whenever possible. As Pete Smith, MGM's publicity chief, had declared: "I want the girls in action. Get them swimming, running, tossing footballs, any goddamn thing, as long as it's *action*."[17]

As "that wild Diana Medford," Joan happily flaunts her shapely calves as she dances in front of a mirror in the film's opening sequence. She raises a toast: "To myself—I have to live myself until I die, so may I always like—myself!" At a party later, Diana dances on a tabletop, the jazz intoxicating her and the handsome football star Ben Blaine (Johnny Mack Brown), who, like many of Joan's costars, is hypnotized by her legs. Diana's friend

~ ABOVE *Joan with her close friend William Haines, in* Spring Fever *(1927).*

~ OPPOSITE *In* Our Modern Maidens *(1929) with Anita Page.*

Ann (Anita Page) embodies the dark side of the force, seducing Ben into marriage at the behest of her gold-digging mama.

Joan in despair would always be a singular sight. Here, at the close of the silent era, disconsolate at the prospect of losing Ben, she knits her brows in exasperation, and her eyes grow dark with jealousy and dreadful thoughts. But, like the Diana of mythology, she is indeed a huntress and, in a final public confrontation with Ann, it is she who retains her dignity, and an inebriated Ann who tumbles down a flight of stairs to her death. The studio promptly doubled Joan's salary. "I'd drive around with a small box camera," said Joan, "taking pictures of 'Joan Crawford' in lights."[18]

For the next three years, Joan was identified with such roles—bright young "moderns" with a passion for bacchanalian parties and flesh-flashing dances. The "sequels" included *Our Modern Maidens* (1929), *Our Blushing Brides* (1930), and *Dance, Fools, Dance* (1931). As Diana says in *Our Dancing Daughters*, "It's such a pleasant thing—just to be alive!"

*Our Modern Maidens* was released in August 1929, three months after Joan's marriage to "Doubles" in New York, where they spent their honeymoon at the Algonquin Hotel. *Our Modern Maidens* celebrated the apotheosis of the Jazz Age, with Joan's frothy, unsophisticated Billie Brown leaving school and finding love and the thrill of the dance. Fairbanks plays her hush-hush fiancé, and when he smothers her face and neck with kisses, the enjoyment of both partners is obvious. "She did her makeup beautifully," recalled Fairbanks. "No one could have done it better. Her eyes, lips, and cheekbones were exaggerated, and she

～ OPPOSITE *Joan in* Untamed *(1929), with the statuesque Gwen Lee.*

～ ABOVE *With Robert Montgomery in* Untamed *(1929).*

knew how to exaggerate them even more."[19] Billie's zest and flightiness are reflected in her flamboyant clothes and jewelry. "I had one spectacular scene, a solo dance in a costume by Adrian—my first—and [Douglas Fairbanks Jr.] had a scene where he accurately impersonated John Barrymore, John Gilbert and Douglas Senior."[20]

*Untamed* opened in December 1929. Hampered by long, declamatory scenes aboard ship, as Joan's character Bingo returns to New York with her guardians and ready to inherit prodigious "oil interests," *Untamed* showed that Joan possessed a fresh-faced, naturalistic style of acting far removed from the doll-like expression of many stars and starlets of the 1920s. She could sing, and she could dance with undulating sensuality, flashing her thighs and a snow-white smile. Bingo clawed and kicked any man who tried to paw her.

One rival stood in her path. Norma Shearer was two years older than Joan, and her husband was Irving Thalberg, the head of MGM production. Shearer embodied the refinement that Joan could only aspire to, and could only acquire by dint of application during the 1930s. "I resented the hell out of Norma Shearer," exclaimed Joan in old age."[21] "They were complete opposites," recalled Frederica Sagor Maas, a screenwriter at the studio. "As warm and outgoing as Norma was, Joan was cold and reserved. Norma was generous in spirit; Joan was calculating."[22] The most damning proof of Shearer's hold over her husband and boss came with her being cast in *A Free Soul* (1931). Adela Rogers St. Johns had scripted the film with

Joan in mind, and she urged Thalberg to give her the role. But Shearer, fresh from her Oscar in *The Divorcee* (1930), asserted her authority, and Thalberg assigned the role to his wife.[23] No wonder Joan turned always to Louis B. Mayer, and rarely to Thalberg. Mayer was quite simply her mentor, "the man who has helped me most in my career," as she reiterated through the years.[24] Not until Hurrell embarked on a series of photos of Joan in 1930, portraits that stripped her of glamour, could the younger star challenge Shearer for dramatic roles at MGM. Joan's innate savvy already told her that she should not compete with sex symbols like Clara Bow or the young Jean Harlow. Instead she decided to focus on maturing as an actress, and thus prepared the way for a durable career—one that would survive the stock-market crash of 1929, the Great Depression, and World War II. It marked the end of her beginning.

~ ABOVE, CLOCKWISE FROM TOP LEFT *Joan in a dancing frock of pale green chiffon trimmed with panne velvet flowers in a darker shade of green; in* The Understanding Heart *(1927); wearing an Adrian dress of tulle with rhinestone trimmings and ostrich feathers; taken while making* Our Blushing Brides *(1930).*

~ OPPOSITE *Ca. 1928.*

~ OPPOSITE *After filming* Sally, Irene and Mary *(1925)*.

~ ABOVE *Joan in* Our Dancing Daughters *(1928)*.

~ ABOVE *Joan held the "high kick" record on the MGM lot.*

~ OPPOSITE *Just prior to shooting* The Taxi Dancer *(1927), MGM was promoting Joan as an "aesthetic dancer."*

~ ABOVE *Joan, aged 22 and already an MGM star in waiting.*

~ OPPOSITE *In a suit of white flannel after filming* The Understanding Heart *(1927).*

~ ABOVE *Note how Joan for a period liked to leave the tips of her nails uncolored. Photo by George Hurrell, 1928.*

~ OPPOSITE *Wearing a suit "made in the Russian manner," according to the MGM press release.*

~ *All bracelets and earrings to give that peasant-girl look.*

~ *Joan's habitual ankle-straps seem to have been air-brushed out of this studio shot.*

~ *Joan's haunted look here prefigures her postwar gaze.*

~ *Adrian would often joke that his entire reputation as a designer rested on Joan's shoulders!*

~ OVERLEAF *White fur became Joan like no other. Photos by George Hurrell.*

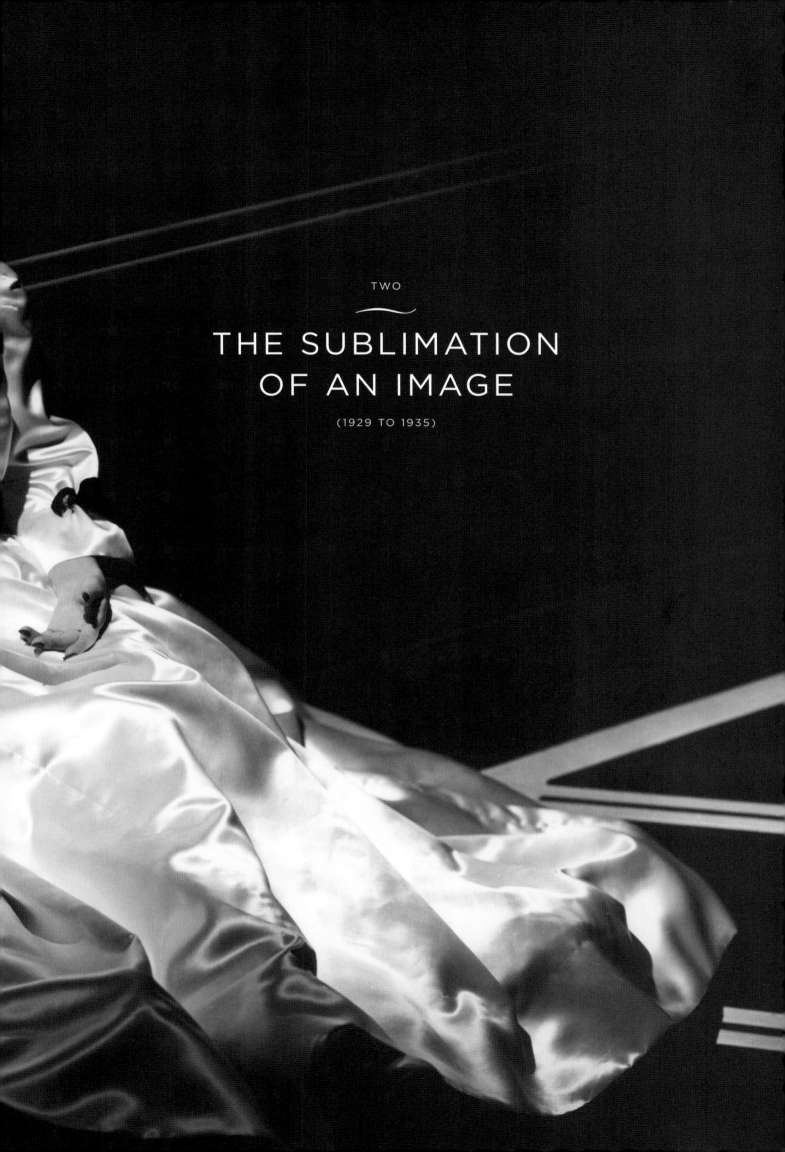

TWO

THE SUBLIMATION
OF AN IMAGE

(1929 TO 1935)

*"England may have had its king and queen,*
*but the United States had its royalty too,*
*and that royalty was us."*

JOAN CRAWFORD

T HE WALL STREET CRASH of 1929 exerted little impact on Hollywood, although producers would learn to focus on working-class heroines rather than spoiled little rich girls. The studios were still profiting from the novelty of sound, and MGM's annual target of fifty films per year seemed reasonable. War and economic recession remained the two conditions for a thriving film industry throughout the twentieth century.

The ensuing three years proved the most crucial in Joan's life and career. She began the 1930s by finally being invited to Pickfair. But if her marriage to Douglas Jr. seemed a dazzling success, akin to that of Tom Cruise and Nicole Kidman many years later, two meetings would change the course of Joan's affections. One was with Franchot Tone, the other with Clark Gable.

Even more significant was the transformation of her screen image, which may be ascribed to the genius of one man—Gilbert Adrian, who had joined MGM in 1928 as a costumier par excellence. Persuaded by composer Irving Berlin to design a Broadway revue at the age of just eighteen, Adrian also caught the eye of Rudolph Valentino and his wife, Natacha Rambova. Contracts with Cecil B. DeMille and then MGM followed swiftly. At twenty-five, Adrian was earning $500 a week at Metro, and by the late 1920s had established himself as the successor to Erté as Hollywood's leading costume designer. Garbo, Shearer, and Crawford were dressed by Adrian with such panache that a generation of filmgoers would revel in their image.

Adrian dressed Joan for the first time in *Our Modern Maidens* (1929), accentuating her lithe, slender legs during a dance sequence, and

~ OPPOSITE *Sharing coffee at home with her first enduring love, Douglas Fairbanks Jr., 1928.*

~ PREVIOUS PAGES *Long gowns tended to make Joan seem taller and more languorous than she was in life. Photo by Laszlo Willinger, 1933.*

endowing her with a junglelike costume featuring broad stripes slashed across white silk. Although a sequel to *Our Dancing Daughters*, the film marked a watershed moment in Joan's career—her last silent picture, and the last salute to the joyous, devil-may-care mood of the flapper age. The pace of studio production may not have been impaired by the stock market crash, but from now on Joan would be cast in roles that accentuated her capacity for hard work and coping with a slim budget.

During the prolific years ahead, Adrian would, little by little, cultivate a new image for Joan, for whom he designed costumes in thirty-one films, the last being *A Woman's Face* in 1941. Adela Rogers St. Johns noted, "Joan wore black a lot in those days, with big picture hats, and much too much makeup. Scarlet lips, mascaraed lashes, flaming hair—hard, haughty, pitifully defiant."[2]

Joan admitted cheerfully that, prior to her bonding with Adrian, she had made most of her own clothes, "and they looked it. I went stockingless while others were experimenting with half-socks. I wore bright red nail polish on fingers and toes, and the minute others did, I switched to pale pink."[3] In short, Joan was dictating fashion, rather than following it. She relished her hair best when natural brown and almost shoulder-length. "I had a big mouth, shoulders wider than John Wayne's, not much in the bosom area, and a lot of bones that showed. The only thing in my favor was my legs. They were beautiful, I admit. And my eyes."[4] Adrian, delighting in those shoulders, would turn them to Joan's advantage—but not until 1932.

As the Depression took hold, fashion was obliged to abandon its exclusive focus on the upper classes. Parisian couturiers such as Jean

Patou continued to dictate trends, but Hollywood reasoned that if everyone wanted to look like Garbo or Shearer or Crawford, their screen clothes must be available to the public in low-cost materials. In 1932, Macy's sold 15,000 copies of the ruffled-shoulder, organdy dress designed by Adrian and worn by Joan in *Letty Lynton*, released that year, and some half a million were purchased nationwide.[5] "Every little girl, all over the country," declared *Vogue*, "within two weeks of the release of Joan Crawford's picture, felt she would die if she couldn't have a dress like that."[6] Adrian "was leading the campaign to make Hollywood a style center for all women, not just to certain women, as Paris had been for years."[7]

Cecil Beaton would write a typically sly description of Joan for *Vogue* in 1931: "Two years ago her hair was fluffed up, and she insisted upon encasing her well-covered body in vulgar costumes with skintight waists and flaring, lampshade fringed skirts, but now she has transformed herself into one of the most brittle, exotic personalities in the colony, with her stark hair brushed to show off her archaic features."[8]

In the autumn of 1932, Joan talked to Adrian about the clothes designed by Elsa Schiaparelli that she had seen during a trip to Paris with Douglas Fairbanks Jr. According to Adrian's biographer, Howard Gutner, on *Today We Live* (1933) she persuaded him "to stress the width of her back rather than try to hide it."[9] Adrian quickly created three dresses featuring squared shoulders and, although inappropriate for the film and for Joan's character, this "new look" would accompany the actress for the rest of her days. As Michael Webb has written, "Adrian popularized the V-shape torso, inspired by

~ ABOVE Today We Live *(1933), with Robert Young and Franchot Tone.*

~ OPPOSITE *A baleful Joan in* Letty Lynton *(1932).*

a hussar's tunic, and padded shoulders and inventive hats, all of which served to focus attention on the actress's face for the all-important close-up."[10]

Irene Sharaff, a gifted costumier in her own right, recalled, "Adrian told me how he had arrived at using shoulder pads, a feature that became like his signature on clothes he designed. It seems that Joan Crawford insisted on feeling absolutely free in her dresses and suits. At fittings she would rotate her shoulders vigorously, with arms outstretched, to test the stretch of the garment across her shoulder blades. As this feeling of unhampered freedom in clothes is possible only in a loose jersey or a sweater, all other fabrics Adrian used for her clothes had to be let out across the back to such an extent that padding was necessary in the shoulders to take up the slack. The result accentuated her broad and angular shoulders."[11]

Adrian also recognized that the way to accentuate Joan's large eyes was to endow her with striking millinery. No hat seemed too outlandish. In *Today We Live* Joan's upper-crust Englishwoman affects the peekaboo hat that, eight years later, would make Michèle Morgan famous in Marcel Carné's *Port of Shadows*. In *Dancing Lady*, also released in 1933, Joan adopts a black pillbox hat, along with black satin gloves— no actress wore so many gloves as Joan throughout the 1930s.

By 1934, the Production Code, drafted in 1930, was finally being enforced by the industry. Ironically, Joan's back could be revealed in all its breadth and beauty in a film like *No More Ladies* (1935), while her bosom—adequate if never ample—had to be concealed. She determined to appear taller than she actually was, and so posture

~ OPPOSITE *George Hurrell would take literally hundreds of photographs of Joan with Clark Gable, seen here in costumes for* Possessed *(1931).*

~ ABOVE *Joan still leading the chorus line, in* Dance, Fools, Dance *(1931).*

proved key. "I always held my head looking up so I could be my full height and a bit more."[12]

In *Susan and God* (1940), she sports a box-hat that, with its all-encompassing wide-mesh veil, suggests that Joan's Susan Trexel has taken a course in beekeeping. Her daughter tells her that she looks divine. "And why not," retorts Joan, "I work like a Trojan at it." (Douglas Fairbanks Jr. described how each day Joan "would massage her whole body, especially her face, with ice cubes."[13])

Couture could play a dramatic function in Crawford's films, thanks principally to Adrian but also to intelligent direction. In *Possessed* (1931), Marian's glossy fur wrap slides sensually to the floor as she embraces Mark and they decide to have sex instead of rushing out to a formal dinner. In *Letty Lynton,* Adrian clothes his star for the murder sequence in a black fur stole, a black coat, and

a black skullcap hat, giving her an aura of death and implacability. In *Dance, Fools, Dance* (1931), Joan poses as a cabaret dancer in order to trap Gable's gangster, Jake Luva; Adrian provides her with a skimpy lamé dress, enabling her to show her legs to full advantage as she taps out her dance of beguilement.

Her profusion of clothes and jewels in this richest period of Joan's career underlines her role as the "kept woman" in, for example, *Possessed* and *Chained* (1934).

Seeing Joan sweep across the screen in gowns by Adrian thrilled her fans, but the popularity of the designs was due in large degree to the still portraits that MGM would send by the hundreds to magazines and newspapers throughout the country. A quick comparison of studio stills of the 1990s and the 1930s demonstrates how

∿ LEFT AND OPPOSITE
*The peekaboo hat suited Joan
down to her high heels.*

much more value Hollywood placed on this kind of publicity during the prewar period. Hurrell, along with Clarence Bull, was arguably the finest practitioner of portrait photography on the West Coast. Trained at art school, he earned an early living as a society photographer. By 1929 he had attracted the attention of Norma Shearer with his stunning images of Ramon Novarro, and moved to MGM, where he occupied the post of still photographer vacated by Ruth Harriet Louise.

Hurrell met Joan in early 1930. An outstanding craftsman by any yardstick, he would describe her as "the most decorative subject I have ever photographed. There is a strength and vitality about her that prevails even in the finished print. If I were a sculptor, I would be satisfied with just doing Joan Crawford all the time."[14] Hurrell shot thirty-three sittings with Joan, including four

glorious sessions in the spring of 1930, which were featured in *Theatre Magazine*, an elegant periodical published on the East Coast.[15]

Hurrell's portraits of Joan, notes Ross Woodman, involved "a new kind of feminine nudity, a nudity of face and stance that thrust itself forward with what [John] Kobal has described as an 'intense, almost masculine energy.'"[16] Hurrell, patient and meticulous, liked to visit Joan's house on North Bristol Avenue in Brentwood Park and follow her from room to room. "His camera was on wheels," recalled Joan. "How he used to move that camera, shoot the picture, and move the key light with it, I'll never know! He looked like an octopus! But it all got there!"[17] They would work through the day and if, by four o'clock, Hurrell himself was tiring, Joan would urge him to continue for another hour or two. "Let's get one more,

*Publicity still for* Letty Lynton *(1932). Photo by George Hurrell.*

Dancing Lady *(1933),*
*photo by George Hurrell.*

just for luck," she instructed him.[18] Such days would yield as many as 150 negatives. Hurrell took more photographs of Joan than of any other star, even Garbo and Shearer. "She liked to pose," he said. "She was very pliable. She gave so much to the stills camera.... She'd spend a whole day, changing maybe into twenty different gowns, different hairdos, changing her makeup, changing everything."[19] For him, Joan possessed "the closest face to Garbo's, to perfect proportions."[20] Apparently, the only problem with her features involved her "right rear jaw, which was a little heavier, and the bridge of her nose, which was so slender that it could make her nostrils look too large."[21]

When Hurrell departed from MGM, Joan requested he continue photographing her—and so he did throughout the 1930s. Such stills were for Joan the essential concomitant of her films. In his eloquent eulogy at Joan's memorial service in 1977,

George Cukor praised "her face, that extraordinary sculptural construction of line and planes, finely chiseled like the mask of some classical divinity from fifth-century Greece. It caught the light superbly, so that you could photograph her from any angle, and her face moved beautifully.... The camera saw, I suspect, a side of her that no flesh-and-blood lover ever saw."[22]

Joan relished the speed of filming in Hollywood at the turn of the new decade. Top stars today may complete at most one or two films each year, such is the time required for postproduction in an effects-driven era. But during the 1920s and 1930s, Joan was no more prolific than other stars—four features in 1929, three in 1930, four in 1931, and three in 1932.

This relentless pace demanded inventiveness and diversity from an actress. Joan, who later in her career would become almost typecast as the

strong-willed, suffering woman, could in her heyday flit from comedy to melodrama, from musical to gangster movie. "No matter what the role or what the picture, I was driven to do my utmost, as if by a whip," she noted in her autobiography.[23] Joan's first release of the new decade, in March 1930, was *Montana Moon*, a sly if often tedious dig at the western genre. To some extent, she had still not found her unique screen personality. Mick LaSalle has observed the way she used to imitate other actresses in her early performances. "In *Montana Moon*, for example, she has a scene where she is flat-out doing Marion Davies."[24] At other moments, Joan keeps her lips apart and flashes the toothy smile associated with Gloria Swanson. Corny and tongue-in-cheek, this spoof on the B Western genre matches Joan as a rich man's daughter with Johnny Mack Brown as Larry, the cowboy

from Montana. "We're as different as velvet and cactus," he drawls, disconcerted by her flirtatious appeal. Joan's most outrageous intervention comes as she sings in a high-pitched screech, startling a group of snoozing cowpokes into wakefulness. When they marry, and move to the big city, Larry finds himself out of tune with the decadent hours kept by his wife's friends, and knocks down a guy who dances suggestively with Joan. She throws him out, has second thoughts, then decides finally to leave him but is borne off on horseback by a masked Larry after he and his pals have held up her father's train. All good rough-and-tumble, but interesting for its revelation of Joan's ability to raise a laugh in the most absurd of circumstances.

*Paid*, released in the very last days of 1930, confirmed her versatility. It was, she felt, "my first really heavy dramatic role, and I did a good job, a

damned good job, thanks to [director] Sam Wood and a script by Charlie MacArthur."[25] The dejection that followed the Wall Street crash of 1929 infiltrates this cynical little movie about a woman, sent to jail in error, who reemerges to take revenge on society through a blackmailing scam. Joan's face haunts the screen from the opening shots, as she stares up at the judge while he pronounces a verdict of grand larceny. The face looks gaunt and undernourished, the eyes bulge wildly. The hair, wavy, is drawn back severely from the ears. The voice is low and throaty, almost like Garbo's. The character of Mary Turner in Paid may be the most naturalistic of all Joan's roles during the 1930s. Not once can she dazzle, or play the brilliant hostess. The mood is sordid, and Mary is perceived as a tramp in the eyes of lovers and the law alike. Charles Rosher's camera stares down at her in

judgment, emphasizing her low-slung breasts and modest height (five feet three inches... or was it four, or even five—nobody seems to agree on that). Tormented by guilt, Mary escapes a second term in jail thanks to a police ruse and the timely confession of professional criminal Joe Garson (Robert Armstrong). Joan had inherited the part when Norma Shearer became pregnant, and she seized her chance with aplomb, shedding the social graces she had started to assume in so many earlier films.

Alert to the commercial acumen of her mentor Louis B. Mayer, Joan did not forsake the effervescent comedies that had brought her so many millions of fans. Dance, Fools, Dance was the first of eight films Joan would make with Gable. Their off-screen affair lasted half a lifetime, but never acquired the notoriety of, say, that of Hepburn and Tracy. Joan was twenty-seven, Gable had just

turned thirty. She was still married to Douglas Fairbanks Jr., he to the forty-seven-year-old theater manager Josephine Dillon. Discretion proved a necessity. Already, in May 1931, a reporter from *Photoplay* wrote that Joan's "heart was empty. And to Joan, an empty heart meant she must seek a new tenant."[26] Fairbanks adored his life with Joan, but his philandering at first perplexed and then infuriated her.

Joan implied on several occasions that Gable was the greatest love of her life. Even her profound affection for Alfred Steele lacked that carnal intensity. Theirs was, she declared, "a glorious affair, and it went on a lot longer than anybody knows. Even though we usually knew our marriages wouldn't last, we were awfully skittish about making any more commitments."[27] Their friendship endured, even in the wake of Gable's

most terrible loss. When the greatest love of *his* life, Carole Lombard, died in a plane crash, Gable visited Joan for consolation and advice. Both came from Middle America, "both peasants by nature," said Joan, "not too well educated, and so frightened and insecure we felt sort of safe and home again when we could get together."[28] In some respects they differed from each other. Joan was usually attracted to fresh-faced types (especially those who danced well), and indeed all four of her husbands could be described as "gentlemen." Gable, however, fascinated her with his rough male demeanor and coarse-cut approach to life. Reputedly, he suffered from severe halitosis, something that must have shocked Joan, for whom cleanliness meant even more than godliness.

She welcomed anything that legitimately prolonged their time together. "When still-

*Two Hurrell portraits of Joan with Gable.*

*Cradling her dying brother (William Bakewell) in* Dance, Fools, Dance *(1931).*

photographer George Hurrell took pictures of us," she said, "he'd simply have the lights set up. Sometimes we were oblivious of the fact that he'd finished shooting."[29] Talking on British television in 1968, she described Gable's primary attraction as "Balls—he had 'em!" and she pointed down suggestively.[30] Joan's salty language could always get to the heart of the matter.

Stardom may have been Joan's lodestone, but independence was always her primary bliss. She sensed that Gable, the epitome of robust virility, would be her equal and more in any domestic arrangement. Her first three husbands were gentlemen, softer than she. Each may have grumbled about the greater glamour and higher pay accorded Joan, yet each acquiesced in the situation. Gable, however, remained beyond her orbit, a star of equal magnitude whose onscreen partnership

enhanced her own brilliance without ever threatening to eclipse it.

Joan asked Louis B. Mayer to cast Gable as the gangster, Jake Luva, in *Dance, Fools, Dance*. It was essentially a supporting role, for the now-forgotten Lester Vail enjoyed the romantic lead, eventually securing the love of Joan's Bonnie Jordan. For MGM, the film seemed a glib means of expiating any guilt the studio had felt at making frothy comedies at the time of the stock-market crash. Bonnie's father loses everything in the debacle, and promptly succumbs to a heart attack. Bonnie, spoiled with every luxury imaginable (including an electric hair dryer aboard her father's ship) must now forage for survival. Hired as a cub reporter on a Chicago newspaper, she shares a one-room apartment with her ineffectual brother, who has fallen in with the notorious Luva

~ *Joan in* This Modern Age
*(1931).*

(clearly based on Al Capone). Bonnie, assigned to investigating the gangland scene, infiltrates Jake's entourage. She "poses" as a cabaret dancer, tap dancing with all her heart in a skimpy lamé dress, displaying her legs to full advantage. Luva is more than amused, and tries to seduce her in his hideout, where Joan shows another side of her talent by pounding out a jazzed-up version of the "Moonlight" sonata on the piano. In a climactic shootout, her brother redeems himself by shooting down Jake, but dies himself in the crossfire, leaving Bonnie to find consolation in the arms of Lester Vail's playboy, Bob Townsend.

Once again, Joan oscillates between mirth and despair, showing an acting range that would be denied her by critics and journalists not even born when *Dance, Fools, Dance* was made. Loyalty was also beginning to emerge as a fundamental attribute of Joan's character on screen. Bonnie's

brother may be feckless, but she never abandons him. Joan behaves in the same key in *This Modern Age* (1931), when she sees her divorced mother rejected by high society.

Joan proved a shrewd—and opportunistic—judge of studio politics. Just as she had gleefully replaced Norma Shearer in *Paid*, so now she leapt at the chance to play Val in *This Modern Age*. Beneath the frothy banter, *This Modern Age* passed severe judgment on contemporary sexual politics. Val Winters sails to Paris to meet a mother she has not seen since infancy. Diane, the mother, develops into the film's most complex character—the mistress of a wealthy aristocrat who retains her dignity in the face of social disapproval. When Val is courted by Neil Hamilton's Bob, she finds his parents condescending and ultraconservative—and appalled by her mother's status as a kept woman.

~ *The film featured Joan with a blonde rinse.*

If Pauline Frederick's demure, controlled portrayal of the mother predominates, Joan once again offers a sturdy performance, gullible yet full of gumption. She has blond hair, and behaves as she must have done when first visiting Pickfair. Her eyebrows are finely arched, not as severe as in other films of the period, and she adumbrates the philosophy of the Jazz Age when she tells Bob: "Make virtues of all your vices, never take anything seriously, and always be amusing."

Luxuriantly dressed, rising at noon, and surrounded by frivolous friends, Joan seemed in this production to be retreating from the new realism. But within the year, she had embarked on another film that reflected the grind of the Depression era, *Possessed*. From the outset, Joan acts without the slightest pretension. She's a factory girl named Marian, set to marry Wallace Ford's brash, insensitive concrete worker. Director Clarence Brown observes them in a prolonged tracking shot as they leave the factory, pass another bickering couple, and seem anchored in the grim urban sprawl.

The studio had come to terms with economic realities. Joan could still be seen in furs and bracelets, but now she had to acquire them either by hard graft, or, as in *Possessed*, by sheer chance. A train trundles through the small town of Erie, and Joan, gazing up at its bright-lit windows, is dazzled by the symbolic tableau of wealth and pleasure—dancing couples, evening dress... When one gracious sugar daddy offers her a glass of champagne, she takes it as one would a business card—her initiation into a world of luxury.

Changed forever, she abandons Erie and her boyfriend ("My life belongs to *me*!" she exclaims), and heads for New York. There, yet another haphazard meeting brings her together with Clark Gable's Mark Whitney. He, a prosperous lawyer

～ OPPOSITE *Joan clutching one of her beloved gardenias, in* Possessed *(1931). Photo by George Hurrell.*

～ ABOVE *The chemistry between Joan and Gable was as evident on screen as it was in private life,* Possessed *(1931).*

(and divorced), declines to marry her. Instead, he takes her as his mistress, beguiled by her candor in admitting she's only after his money. Three years pass, and Joan is ordering from the caterer in fluent French, and arranging large dinner parties (just as she had been doing in real life with Douglas Fairbanks Jr.). She now speaks with a posh, assured accent, clipping her consonants in the manner of Garbo, and playing the piano with elegant aplomb. Adrian endows her with a black evening dress with a low-cut vee, emphasizing the breadth and splendor of her shoulders. Gentility becomes her, and she learns how to dispense with an excess of hats or jewelry.

At certain junctures in all these films, Joan radiated sex appeal. She did not "ooze," like Clara Bow or Jean Harlow; nor did she smolder like Marlene Dietrich. She passes her tongue over her lower lip in anticipation, excitement. She waits,

waits, and then, to her chosen one, she yields with a swooning laugh. When she accepts a kiss from Wallace Ford in *Possessed*, for example, she arches her head back, swanlike, bordering on the imperious.

Joan never denied her simple background off the screen, and neither did her onscreen characters. "Common! That's what I am, common!" she hurls at Wallace Ford's Al, and confesses that she is not Gable's wife but his mistress. It was the smart thing to do during the Depression, and Joan's fan base broadened by the day. Such a scene justifies Mick LaSalle's observation that "In many of [Joan's] films, there's a moment in which her manner falls away, and she suddenly reveals a core of scalding bitterness. In those moments, she never rings false."[31]

In *Possessed* she again concludes on a note of vehement devotion, standing up during an election meeting to admit her relationship with Gable's would-be governor. Her voice is cleverly magnified

~ ABOVE *Joan appeared briefly in* The Hollywood Revue of 1929.

~ OPPOSITE *Joan awaiting her call during the shoot of* Laughing Sinners *(1931)*.

to give a sense of the huge assembly hall and the vigor of her devotion. In fact, the entire sequence is uncannily prescient of *Citizen Kane* (1941), with blackmailers in the balcony staring down at Gable during his speech just as Ray Collins gazes at Kane during his election rally. In both films, the candidate is undone by sexual innuendo.

*Possessed* was the first of Joan's films to be directed by Clarence Brown, who had established his reputation with Garbo vehicles like *Flesh and the Devil, A Woman of Affairs,* and *Anna Christie.* His finesse enhances such moments as the spontaneous embrace between Mark and Marian, when he allows Joan's fur wrap to slither sensually to the floor as the couple's dinner plans are abandoned for something more desirable … No other single shot communicates the manifest chemistry that fired Joan and Gable during these first ardent months of their affair.

## COPING WITH THE DEPRESSION

*"She labors twenty-four hours a day to keep her name in the pupil of the public eye."*
—HEDDA HOPPER[32]

Joan had sworn allegiance to MGM, but she also felt devoted to Hollywood as an entity, as an institution. In November 1929, one of the blackest months in the nation's history, she popped up in *The Hollywood Revue of 1929,* which featured more than twenty MGM stars in a high-kicking celebration of the sound medium and of the studio's immense stages. Introduced by Conrad Nagel, Joan stands demurely beside a piano and launches into a fresh-faced, unsophisticated rendering of "I've Got a Feeling for You." Then she segues into a vigorous dance that displays her perfect legs and litheness of movement. As Nagel says so obsequiously, "She's the personification of youth and beauty and joy

~ *Edmund Goulding directs Joan and John Barrymore in* Grand Hotel *(1932)*.

and happiness." Although not unduly talented as a singer, Joan at one point assigned as much as three hours a day to her singing lessons, as well as riding and practicing polo.[33]

Two years later, Joan appeared in *The Stolen Jools*, in aid of the National Variety Artists union. Paid for by Chesterfield Cigarettes, distributed gratis by Paramount, the film short played throughout the country, and at the end of each screening the audience was urged to contribute toward the union's tuberculosis sanitarium in Saranac Lake, New York. This clumsy yet engaging slapstick extravaganza featured everyone from Gary Cooper to Edward G. Robinson and Laurel and Hardy. Joan is accused of having purloined Norma Shearer's pearls (the offscreen animosity between the stars made this hilariously plausible)—but in fact all she has taken is a poodle.

By early 1932, she could tell an interviewer, "I'm always groping, seeking to learn, trying to improve myself. I want so much to fight off conceit—I must never allow myself to become self-satisfied." But she felt that would not happen. "My ambition is too driving—too relentless to permit me to grow complacent."[34] She felt more at home on the studio stage than she did in many rooms of her own mansion. "To walk on [the set] at nine [A.M.] in a beautiful evening dress, perfectly coiffed, made up to perfection, and the men in dinner jackets, and we start playing a love scene. That's pretty exciting," she told John Kobal in later life.[35] "And some of it rubs off, you know."

At the age of twenty-seven (twenty-three in the public eye), Joan needed a fresh challenge. She had proved that she could carry a film on her redoubtable shoulders. Now, in late 1932, she

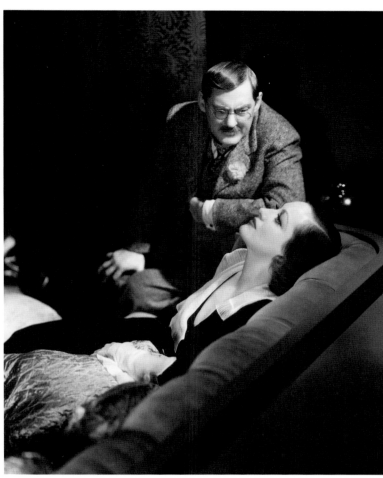

would at last have the opportunity to test her mettle against the finest talent Hollywood could offer. Vicki Baum's archetypal novel *Grand Hotel* was acquired for the screen by MGM, and Garbo immediately cast as Grusinskaya, the legendary Russian dancer who joins other guests in a five-star Berlin hotel. The male parts were quickly assigned to the heavyweight actors of the day: John Barrymore as the Baron von Geigern, Wallace Beery as the brutal business mogul, Preysing, and Lionel Barrymore as his book-keeper, the ailing Kringelein.

The battle for the only other female role of any consequence was as relentless and highly publicized as the search for Scarlett O'Hara in *Gone with the Wind* later in the decade. Marlene Dietrich, Mae West, Tallulah Bankhead, and Marie Dressler were all considered. When Mayer and Thalberg decided to give Joan the part of Flaemm-chen, the saucy stenographer who would attract the three leading men in turn, Garbo bridled. She told Mayer that she would not shoot a single scene with her rival, and threatened to return to Sweden if her wish was not respected. She even insisted that Joan not start shooting her scenes until after 5 P.M., when Garbo would have left the stages.

Joan, however, refused to buckle under such pressure. At first reluctant to accept a supporting role, she acknowledged that to play a working-class girl on the make would please her fans. She also reveled in the prospect of appearing alongside Garbo, and even in her autobiography the circumstances acquired a roseate, almost mystical hue. "She was a fascinating actress whom I adored from a distance," wrote Joan, and described the moment when Garbo, trudging upstairs to her

~ Grand Hotel (1932), *Adrian designed an outfit that Joan's Flaemmchen could wear both by day and by night. Photos by George Hurrell.*

dressing room after a day on the set, crossed paths with Joan as she was preparing to begin the long night's shooting. "Suddenly above me was that beautiful face with those compelling eyes, and the woman I'd thought so aloof was saying: 'I'm so sorry we are not working together. What a pity, eh? Our first picture together and not one scene.'"[36]

Garbo's fee for the picture was $68,000, and Joan, whose films had performed as well if not better than Garbo's, had to be content with $60,000. The casting could not have been more adroit. As Mick LaSalle has written: "With Garbo, sex was a sacrament. With Shearer, sex was emancipation. With Crawford, sex was a commodity."[37] Flaemmchen ("Little Flame") is on the make from the outset, batting her eyelids insouciantly at the baron from beneath her cloche hat. *Grand Hotel* takes place in the Berlin of the late 1920s, with

ruin and decadence at the door, and an attractive stenographer like Flaemmchen is alert to the main chance. The baron may be diverted by Flaemmchen, but he is infatuated with Grusinskaya, and so Joan must submit to the coarse advances of Preysing, accepting his offer to go to England with him out of sheer expediency. Love, "the real thing," she's told the baron, "just doesn't exist."

Joan endows Flaemmchen with a pragmatic tinge. When Preysing kills the baron after finding he has stolen his wallet, Flaemmchen, hysterical, rushes for help to Kringelein, in whom she recognizes goodness—but also a meal ticket. It's a full-blooded performance, more cogent, more naturalistic than Garbo's as the recalcitrant ballerina whose simple line, "I want to be alone," would enter legend. Joan absorbed every scene, every comment made by director Edmund Goulding

~ OPPOSITE Letty Lynton (1932).

~ ABOVE Letty Lynton (1932), Joan with Louise Closser Hale, playing her maid. "We're taking that boat home from Montevideo."

("You've grown quiet, you've gained strength, Joan"[38]) She was impressed most of all by Lionel Barrymore. "His performance as the shabby, abject Kringelein, with only a short while to live, ran the gamut from comedy to profound pathos," she wrote in 1962.[39]

Adrian surpassed himself designing gowns for both actresses. Joan beguiles Barrymore with what would today be termed a cocktail dress. It exposed her bosom and, in Alexander Walker's phrase, "her creamy yoke of collar-bone."[40] The white collars, cuffs, and gloves contrasted with the severe black silk crepe of the dress itself. It suggests, says Howard Gutner, "a domestic—a working girl—whereas the plunging neckline suggests something much more intimate."[41] *Grand Hotel* became the most lavish and ambitious Hollywood production since the coming of sound. Its

$700,000 budget, obese for the period, proved to be justified, for the film earned at least four times that amount during its initial release. The basic format created by Vicki Baum—a group of individuals brought together by chance under one luxurious roof—would be emulated on several occasions by the cinema, most recently in *Bobby* (2006).

*Letty Lynton*, opening just eighteen days after *Grand Hotel*, confirmed once and for all Joan's abilities as a dramatic actress. She plays the moneyed, well-raised single girl enjoying a sojourn in Montevideo before cruising back to New York. Nils Asther plays Emile, the passionate, persistent Latin lover, intent on sweeping Letty off her elegantly shod feet. "Oh, don't talk!" she tells him in a throaty murmur, "just listen to the music..." She is given to dreamy gestures, and her burgeoning romance with Hale Darrow (Robert Montgomery)

during the trip home offers Adrian the opportunity to dress her in ermine wraps, and that soon-to-be-famous organdy-ruffed dress, to match her feckless mood.

Joan could play such scenes in her sleep, but the boulevard humor and effervescent tone of the first half of *Letty Lynton* scarcely prepares us for the second half. The elegance of Letty's existence is soon undermined by a filigree of pain. Emile appears on the quay in New York, and pursues her with an almost manic obsession. He tries to blackmail her with the love letters she has written him in the past. A distraught Letty resolves to poison this importunate lover, and visits him in his rooms. The *crime passionel* is unsettling in its naturalism, with Emile beating Letty in frustration, and then swallowing the poison by mistake, for she has on a whim poured it into her own glass

instead of his. He dies in a prolonged agony while Letty tries, clumsily, to cover her tracks. Joan brilliantly communicates the tide of remorse that engulfs this heroine, whose cosseted life has kept the world's ugly underside at bay until this point. She's especially persuasive in the scenes with her mother, whose shadow Letty tries to evade and yet whose false testimony will in the end save her from the gallows. It's as if film noir had merged with romantic comedy.

Then, out of the blue, came *Rain* (1932). Seven years earlier, Joan had already slipped, unnoted, into an earlier adaptation of Somerset Maugham, *The Circle*, but *Rain* had mutated far beyond Maugham's grasp. A tart, sardonic tale of the South Seas that Maugham so loved, the short story "Miss Thompson" had been written in 1916 while Maugham was staying in Hong Kong. Then in 1922,

~ ABOVE   Rain *(1932), with Walter Huston as the hypocritical and sex-starved preacher.*

~ RIGHT   *Joan with her beloved Clark Gable, on the set of* Possessed *(1931).*

John Colton and Clemence Randolph had adapted it for the Broadway stage under the title *Rain*. Screen rights to the play were sold to United Artists in 1923 for $150,000, in those days a prodigious sum for a literary original (although only 25 percent went to Maugham). Five years later, Gloria Swanson played the lusty prostitute, Sadie Thompson, in a screen version under the direction of Raoul Walsh.

Lewis Milestone, still basking in the triumph of first *All Quiet on the Western Front* (1930) and then *The Front Page* (1931), directed *Rain* for United Artists. Louis B. Mayer had reluctantly loaned his female star to a rival studio, and Joan discovered how much she missed the attendant genii of Cedric Gibbons and Adrian. Throughout her life she would look upon *Rain* as an aberration, and critics both ancient and modern have agreed, with gusto. As Alexander Walker wrote, with percep-

tion, "It was probably the way he [Milestone] revealed the male will inside Sadie's assertively female body...which proved too unexpected a charge for contemporary fans to accept."[42]

For some reason, Joan felt drawn to the story. She already knew well how disdainful the privileged classes, and how condescending the nouveaux riches, could be. So the notion of a prostitute from the red-light district of Honolulu driving a zealous missionary to his death held a strong allure, and seemed like a lot of fun at the time.

The flavor of Maugham's original seemed even more diminished in Maxwell Anderson's screenplay. Milestone's ponderous direction fetters the fantasy that in the story encompasses so much of the humid atmosphere of Samoa. And yet anyone viewing the film today must admire the charisma of Joan's performance and the way she

embodies Maugham's description of Sadie as "plump, and in a coarse fashion pretty," as well as "loud-voiced and garrulous" and "brazen, brazen," as the missionary's wife affirms. Her costumes were assembled, rather than designed, by a friend of Adrian's, Milo Anderson, who would not receive a credit on the film. Joan wore everything with vulgar aplomb: openwork stockings, bangles and bells, a lightweight, gingham-check dress that seems painted around her generous hips, and even a severe black suit to signal her temporary conversion at the hands of the minister. Her makeup exceeded even Swanson's in *Sadie Thompson*. Her eyes, black-rimmed with kohl like a latter-day Theda Bara or Pola Negri, leap from the faux-naif, inquiring face. Her hair is curly and voluminous. She drinks her booze straight from the bottle, and she dangles a cigarette from her mouth with that

lazy suggestiveness that Marlene Dietrich would later bring to her cameo in *Touch of Evil* (1958). Her finest moment comes when Reverend Davidson tells her that she cannot sail on to Sydney, and that the missionary insists she be sent back to San Francisco to face trial for her "sins." Joan's face is that of a woman whose reprieve from the death sentence has been denied.

Joan's Miss Thompson may be a caricature, as indeed Maugham surely intended, but her character throbs with a lust for life's sensations that renders those around her stiff and moribund.

During this prolific period, Joan's private life seemed also in a state of constant flux. She had divorced Douglas Fairbanks Jr. in May 1933, she had met and would presently wed Franchot Tone, and she remained infatuated with Clark Gable. Sex for Joan could aspire to romantic ritual, but it was

also a physical need, to be accommodated, like shopping or the hairdresser, in her daily agenda (usually one hour in the afternoon). She kept her body in excellent condition, taking ice-cold showers, subjecting herself to rigorous massage sessions, swimming, and even (prior to her first marriage) sleeping on a screened porch. "As a dancer," she recalled, "I could leap the highest and jump the farthest."[43] Alcohol and cigarettes were still beyond the pale for Joan—at least until the early 1940s. In short, she was committed to physical fitness long before Jane Fonda.

She was never embarrassed by sex. If, between marriages, she held a dinner party at her home in Brentwood Park, she would openly invite her current beau to accompany her upstairs while the other guests departed. Much later, Kirk Douglas would confess to having enjoyed a late-night "quickie" with Joan halfway up her staircase after a date, before accompanying his host to check on the children. Jackie Cooper wrote, with reverence, "She was a very erudite professor of love, a wild woman. She would bathe me, powder me, cologne me."[44]

Each conquest, swift or slow, shored up Joan's heartfelt insecurity. "I *want* to be liked," she told John Kobal. "I want so *desperately* to be liked."[45] The encounters with Gable were snatched furtively, in hotel suites or borrowed apartments, so as to wound neither his nor her spouse. Their affair was probably more exciting, confided Crawford much later in life, "because we felt like kids who'd gotten into the cookie jar while Uncle Louie [Mayer] was in the other room."[46]

In March 1933, some five months after the premiere of *Rain*, Joan's career would return to MGM, with the release of *Today We Live*. On paper,

~ LEFT *Joan starred with many of the top leading men of the 1930s. Here she is with Gary Cooper in* Today We Live *(1933).*

~ OPPOSITE Today We Live *(1933), the cut of the trench coat accentuated Joan's broad shoulders.*

this might have been a masterpiece—directed by Howard Hawks, written by novelist William Faulkner, and costarring heartthrob Gary Cooper and a man who would become the new love of Joan's life, Franchot Tone. In fact, though, Joan gate-crashed the project—or rather MGM insisted she do so, at brutally short notice, obliging Hawks and Faulkner to abandon their macho scenario for a film that would blend romance and action. Irving Thalberg told Hawks that the studio needed to fulfill a $500,000 contractual obligation with Joan, so Faulkner added the character of Ann who loves one man while promising to marry another. Joan "balked at the idea of being in an all-male film, and insisted that Faulkner rewrite her dialogue to match the clipped speech of the men."[47]

Joan plays Diana ("Ann") Boyce-Smith, an upper-crust girl living with her brother Ronnie

(Tone) in Kent during World War I. Their father is reported killed at the front, and at the same time an American pilot, Richard Bogard (Cooper), is billeted on their estate. Joan, with a peekaboo hat and hair brushed straight down and curled up at the back, once again intones her lines like a displaced Garbo. Both Ronnie's bosom pal, Claude (Robert Young), and Bogard declare their love for her, in somewhat unconvincing terms. Unconvincing, because as Hawks himself admitted, "It was again our little love theme about two boys who get together."[48]

When Ronnie and Claude embark on military duties for the navy, and Bogard (who has been listed as killed in action) signs up as a bomber pilot over France, Hawks is on more familiar territory. Diana's coincidental arrival in France as an ambulance driver distracts the men, and the film ends on a tragic note as Ronnie and

~ ABOVE *Today We Live (1933), with the blinded Claude (Robert Young), who brings out Joan's tender side.*

~ OPPOSITE *Joan attending a Hollywood premiere with her second husband, Franchot Tone.*

Claude (now blinded), buddies to the end, charge their little torpedo boat relentlessly and selflessly into an enemy cruiser.

Adrian's costumes appear anachronistic, reflecting the couture of the early 1930s rather than 1916, and strengthening the impression that Joan has wandered inconveniently into this hymn to male gallantry. She certainly does not look entranced by Gary Cooper who, gentle by nature, seems incongruous in his role as the macho flyer. Only Franchot Tone escapes with real credit in *Today We Live*, giving Ronnie some mettle beneath his playful, almost effete exterior.

Tone had grown up enveloped in creature comforts, for his father was president of the Carborundum Company, which pioneered electrochemicals for commercial use (and is today a division of BP). Suave and immaculately groomed,

he had graduated Phi Beta Kappa from Cornell. Joan admired his love and knowledge of culture. They would spend evenings together at the opera, the L.A. Philharmonic, and the Hollywood Bowl. He urged her to seek screen roles that would bring her the kind of exalted reputation associated with Eleanora Duse and Sarah Bernhardt.[49]

Louis B. Mayer once again initiated a change of gears in Joan's career. His daughter Irene had recently married David O. Selznick, and in early 1933 Mayer assigned him to produce *Dancing Lady*. The novel by James Warner Bellah traced the rise of a young dancer to stardom over a twenty-year period, but Selznick compressed the narrative into a few months, and also introduced a stronger musical element, perhaps to combat the success that Warners had enjoyed with *42nd Street*. (Bellah would later achieve some immortality with his sto-

ries adapted by John Ford—*Fort Apache, She Wore a Yellow Ribbon,* and *Rio Grande.*)

*Dancing Lady* not only enhanced the on-screen charisma of Joan and Clark Gable, but it also introduced the talents of Fred Astaire. Already established as a star of Broadway and vaudeville, Astaire had been signed by RKO, and the studio agreed to loan him to MGM for a brief appearance in *Dancing Lady*—playing himself.

Once again, Joan is cast as the cheerful, salty, ambitious gal from the wrong side of the tracks. Janie, her character, is arrested by the cops during a raid on a burlesque theater, but a wealthy client, Tod Newton (Tone), notes her lissome legs and rescues her from the judge's wrath. "I'm goin' uptown, and I'm goin' on my own," Janie drawls to her roommate, Rose. Tod's motives are strictly opportunistic, but he makes the error of presenting Janie

to Broadway director Patch Gallagher (Gable), who reluctantly gives her a part in his new musical.

The pleasure of the film derives not from its lightweight romance but rather from the slick approach of Robert Z. Leonard, who had been directing in Hollywood since 1913 and had filmed Garbo in her first screen test in the U.S. There's a delightful montage sequence as Janie pursues Patch through the crowded streets of Manhattan, composed of close-ups of feet and legs and collisions as the two future lovers bump into each other and he tries desperately to avoid her attentions.

Joan must have relished the parallels with her real-life situation. Already beguiled by the charms of Franchot Tone, she was still swept away by the red-blooded masculinity of Clark Gable. Her love of gardenias is indulged by Leonard. At a party chez Tod, she wears a garland of the white

~ *Joan in* Dancing Lady *(1933).*

flowers around her neck, and Tod urges her to join him in Hawaii, where gardenias grow by the million. "The first night we went dancing," Joan recalled in her autobiography, "I wore a collar of gardenias around my throat and he a gardenia in his lapel. The fragrant blooms were my favorite, they meant luck and love, and [Franchot] always had the house and my studio dressing room filled with them."[50]

Tone, so often the handsome, doe-eyed lover, plays the villain in *Dancing Lady*, pushing for Janie's hand in marriage even if it jeopardizes her career as a dancer. He even withdraws his funding to ensure that the show will close after Janie has refused his offer and is clearly becoming involved with Patch.

Joan's prodigious energy is brought to the fore throughout the picture. She swims vigorously

in a fetching one-piece suit and white bonnet, and she makes more than an honorable stab at dancing "Heigh-Ho, the Gang's All Here" alongside an effortless Astaire. In fact, she had sustained a broken ankle but resolved to complete the taxing dance sequence without complaining to the crew. Her tenacity produced results. More than 18,000 people crowded to see *Dancing Lady* in its first day at the Capitol Theater in Manhattan, a record for the period.

Adrian's costumes include a frothy creation in white organdy with voluminous clusters of ostrich feathers over her shoulders and upper arms, but also a rather absurd Bavarian outfit, complete with dirndl and plaits. As Adrian's biographer, Howard Gutner, has written, "*Dancing Lady* is a film that believes ardently in the magic of lucky clothes, and the near-magical transforming

~ Dancing Lady *(1933)*. *Photo by George Hurrell.*

∽ ABOVE *Working at NBC radio, thanks to the influence of her husband Franchot Tone, ca. 1935.*

∽ OPPOSITE Sadie McKee *(1934).*

power of the right garment: clothing as talisman."[51] Janie spends every spare penny on her clothes—from black silk crepe to black wool, from pillbox hats to the ubiquitous white gloves that by now had become a trademark of Joan's collaboration with Adrian.

## SEA CHANGE AND SECOND MARRIAGE

*"Franchot had the patience of a saint, and he was never helped by being Joan Crawford's husband. The industry was cruel; only one star to a family, unless you were terribly, terribly on top."*

—JOAN CRAWFORD[52]

In what, with hindsight, may be regarded as her prime of life, Joan prepared for a second marriage. Franchot Tone would star alongside her in

*Sadie McKee* (1934), but Joan was reluctant to formalize their romance, perhaps because the memory of her divorce was still too fresh. MGM again obliged Joan's fans by presenting Sadie as the cook's daughter who becomes a wealthy kept woman in New York. This time, her youthful sweetheart is played by the strikingly blond Gene Raymond, fresh from his major role in *Flying Down to Rio*, where he had tried, to no avail, to upstage Fred Astaire.

Contemporary fans may not have registered the sea change in Joan's image and comportment. Yet in close-ups her smile was becoming a tad more fixed, her glance more knowing, her voice just that little bit more disposed to condescend. In *Sadie McKee*, she still gives her lower lip an occasional lick of hesitation, but when Franchot Tone asks if she is seriously considering wealthy

~ Sadie McKee (1934), with Gene Raymond as Tommy Wallace, the love of Sadie's teenage years, who ditches her but remains in love until his untimely death from tuberculosis.

~ LEFT *After Sadie has married Jack Brennan she can buy all the clothes she likes (and subscribe to* Variety*)!* RIGHT *Joan posing in Adrian's striking outfit.*

playboy Jack Brennan's proposal of marriage, her response is startling. "What business is it of yours?" she demands, with an imperious scorn not seen hitherto in her personality. As Brennan sinks into a mire of alcoholism, Joan brings to Sadie a surprising measure of assertiveness. Then, finding that her early love, Tommy (Raymond) is on his deathbed, she comforts him at the last in a wrenching scene that gives the lie to those who feel that Joan could not give her soul to a part.

Not surprisingly, when asked by Robert Aldrich which of her old movies her character in *Whatever Happened to Baby Jane?* would like to watch on TV, Joan opted for *Sadie McKee*—especially the close-ups involving her and Gene Raymond. It remains a film that presents her versatility at its best. She performs as a chorus girl, she revels in light comedy, and she struts her stuff as

the mistress of Brennan's household. *Sadie McKee* may have grossed only $838,000 (by comparison with *Dancing Lady*'s $1,490,000), but Joan could now afford to spread her largesse beyond her immediate circle. In December 1933, she "adopted" two rooms at the Presbyterian Hospital on North Vermont Avenue in Los Angeles, asking that they be reserved exclusively for "sick studio staff, technicians, retired actors, bit-parts and fans and other friends who could not afford to pay for themselves."[53] As she would tell John Kobal in the final decade of her life: "I know nothing but gratitude for this fine, great industry that I love and worship."[54]

In *Chained*, Clarence Brown, perhaps the most underrated of prewar Hollywood directors, once more tested Joan's mettle as a serious actress as he had done in *Possessed* and *Letty Lynton*. Her role seems almost too good to be true—a wealthy

young socialite named Diane, who only slightly
resents the fact that she's the spoiled mistress of a
New York business magnate, and who then finds
herself pursued by a lethally handsome rancher
from the Argentine. Dressed to the nines by
Adrian, in a series of gowns worthy of a top fashion model, Joan's Diane Lovering transcends the
image of a contemporary playgirl established in
the opening scene, as she races a speedboat across
the Hudson River.

George Folsey's lighting became her. She
noted "how Folsey often masked the forehead to
direct the light at her eyes, and how he threw a
shadow on her chin and neck, sometimes by plac-
ing leaves at the bottom of the key light."[55] In *The
Gorgeous Hussy* (1936), this technique would become
even more manifest, making the whites of Joan's
eyes gleam like fine porcelain in their clarity.

Joan by now could appear sophisticated on
the one hand (with Adrian's furs emphasizing her
hauteur), and courageous under fire on the other.
When a smirking, brilliantined Clark Gable tries
to impress her onboard a cruise liner bound for
Buenos Aires, Diane proves poised and hard to
ensnare. She matches him in sports, too, excelling
in swimming and clay pigeon shooting. For the
first two thirds of the picture, Diane appears the
most amoral of all Joan's characters to date. She
succumbs to the charms of her Latin lover, riding
and cavorting at his ranch, while back in Buenos
Aires her hotel suite is festooned with flowers
from her sugar daddy in New York.

Then her horizon darkens dramatically. On
returning to Manhattan, she learns that Otto
Kruger's sensitive, adoring Richard is finally being
divorced by his wife. Diane melts at the sight of a

∽ ABOVE *Shipboard romance: Joan and Gable in* Forsaking All Others *(1934).*

∽ OPPOSITE *Hurrell portrait for* Forsaking All Others *(1934).*

wedding ring, and slides into a life of opulence and security without so much as a second thought for Gable. But her coiffure, now severe—austere even—gives Diane the air of a person in mourning. A chance encounter with Gable in a New York gun store brings her dilemma into sharp focus: She is irremediably attracted to the South American and yet she brims with affection for her attentive, if aging husband. Her anguish reaches its peak when Gable bursts into the married couple's country retreat, bent on claiming Diane once and for all. Kruger, perfectly cast as Richard, liberates his wife by giving her an immediate divorce. Such an ending is too glib, too abrupt, but it's one that, flouting the dictates of the Production Code, enables Joan and Gable to find happiness yet again—at least on screen, for in real life Joan must have winced at the similarities between her character's dilemma

and that of her and Gable, each at one time married and never "free" to fulfill their love.

At least they could make films together, and the studio reteamed them immediately in *Forsaking All Others* (1934), where once again Gable must pursue a waiting game, while Joan's emotional bond with the fiancé who jilts her slowly withers. Adrian designed the most spectacular of bridal gowns for Joan, with hoops that began at the knees. According to Howard Gutner, the costumier used some forty yards of "eggshell soufflé and rose-point lace," as well as a veil edged in appliquéd lace, and "starched to make it stand away from the head and body." Adrian inserted wire in the high collar so it would remain erect when Joan was moving.[56]

In Englewood Cliffs, New Jersey, on October 11, 1935, Joan at last married Franchot Tone—

～ ABOVE *On and off screen with second husband, Franchot Tone.*

～ OPPOSITE *Hurrell took this shot of Joan and Tone at their home, using just the one light.*

although her apparel was somewhat less grand than her character's in *Forsaking All Others*. She wore a blue wool suit and hat, and carried a bride's bouquet.[57] She seemed desperately anxious to make the marriage work. "What a lovely Christmas we had that year," she recalled. "Franchot gave me a star-sapphire pendant and bracelet. I surprised him with a sixteen-cylinder car which he didn't see until three-thirty Christmas Eve morning, after the guests had gone home."[58] They spent Christmas alone in Brentwood, content with each other's company. Joan's bosom pal William Haines had become a decorator to the stars in Hollywood, and he executed Joan's vision for improving her home. "The drawing room was gardenia-white with Wedgwood-blue corner cabinets, long lovely modern couches

and English antiques."[59] The former dining room became a music room, and Haines was asked to construct a new wing to house a spacious new dining room and kitchen.

Like Fairbanks, Tone was a gentleman to a fault, a consort to Joan's monarch. He loathed the limelight and Joan's habit of mingling with her fans when she arrived at a Hollywood premiere. His discretion dragged at his career like an anchor. MGM gave him starring roles, and he acquitted himself admirably, but he lacked the hunky charisma of a Gable or even a Cooper. Joan and Franchot wanted children ardently, but nature denied them, with Joan suffering at least two miscarriages, or perhaps as many as seven.[60] "A dancer's muscles should be good for childbearing," she said. "They aren't."[61]

~ ABOVE Dance, Fools, Dance *(1931), with Lester Vail.*

~ OPPOSITE *In a black satin gown designed by Adrian.*

~ ABOVE  *Clark Gable, Norma Shearer, Joan, and Douglas Fairbanks Jr. at a Mayfair Club dance in Hollywood in June 1932.*

~ OPPOSITE TOP  *Relaxing with Douglas Fairbanks Jr. Photograph by Clarence Bull for MGM.*

~ OPPOSITE BOTTOM  *With Douglas Fairbanks Jr. and his mother (the first wife of Douglas Fairbanks Sr.).*

～ ABOVE AND OPPOSITE *Photos by George Hurrell, 1935.*

～ OVERLEAF, LEFT **Sadie McKee** *(1934).* RIGHT **Our Blushing Brides** *(1930).*

～ PREVIOUS *A Garboesque Joan with Wallace Beery in* Grand Hotel *(1932). Photograph by George Hurrell.*

～ OPPOSITE *The makeup here gives Joan's face a well-scrubbed, sporty look that belies the formal gown. Photo by George Hurrell, 1930.*

～ ABOVE *MGM studio portrait, taken by George Hurrell in 1930.*

～ OVERLEAF, LEFT *Publicity still for* Letty Lynton *(1932). Photo by George Hurrell.* RIGHT *A 1933 photo by George Hurrell for MGM.*

*~ With the gardenias she wore as a talisman. Photo by George Hurrell, 1931.*

~ OPPOSITE  *The pensive look and, as so often, a bouquet of flowers at hand. Photo by George Hurrell, 1932.*

~ ABOVE  *Photo by George Hurrell, 1931.*

～ ABOVE *One of MGM's most relaxed portraits of Joan. Photo by George Hurrell, 1931.*

～ OPPOSITE *The upstretched arm and the long gown make Joan appear taller and more sensual than ever. Photo by George Hurrell, 1933.*

# A WOMAN OF DISCIPLINE

(1935 TO 1940)

*"I remember every one of my important roles the way*

*I remember a part of my life, because at the time*

*I did them, I was the role and it was*

*my life for fourteen hours a day."*

JOAN CRAWFORD

⌒

N 1935 JOAN WAS TURNING thirty-one, although to her fans she remained just twenty-seven, as per the official biographies and press releases from MGM. During a single decade in Hollywood, she had made thirty-eight films. Together they had grossed more than $35 million, a prodigious sum for the period. Joan's name now belonged firmly "above the title," and would stay so throughout virtually all of the thirty-five years that remained of her career.

But she needed to adapt to changing circumstances. She could no longer take ingénue parts, and fresh faces were surging up through the studio ranks. Screwball comedy appealed to a wide audience, and in *I Live My Life* (1935), Joan may well have been influenced by the performance of Jean Arthur in *The Whole Town's Talking*, released eight months earlier. The screenplay by Joseph

Mankiewicz caught the spirit of the time, painting a light-fingered dalliance between Kay Bentley, a New York socialite (inevitably Joan) and a deceptively languid archaeologist named Terence O'Neill, played by Brian Aherne. They meet on the Greek island of Naxos, and he beguiles her with his flippant talk of Pygmalion, the bachelor god, and his Galatea. As in *Chained* (1934), Joan is immediately depicted as a fresh-air fiend. Adrian dresses her in a white and blue naval top, complete with officer's stripes, ideal for the yachting cruise Kay is making with her entourage in the Cyclades. Spoiled, ineffably rich, she jumps gleefully into a flirtation with Terry. Once home, she admits to the family butler that she is "an exceedingly nasty young woman." Yet this Joan could never be nasty in the way that (the later) Crawford could be. Instead, she keeps her tongue well in cheek, with a

⌒ PREVIOUS *Photo by Laszlo Willinger, 1938.*

⌒ OPPOSITE **The Bride Wore Red** *(1937), Joan preparing for a scene with Robert Young.*

133

～ OPPOSITE *With Fred Keating, her would-be fiancé in* I Live My Life *(1935). Note the sailor-boy top Adrian designed for Joan.*

～ BELOW *With Robert Montgomery, with whom Joan made seven features.*

delicious habit of licking her lower lip as she avoids Terry's mocking gaze, and protests that their love can never work. He, in contrast, regards her privileged world with undisguised scorn. "I didn't kiss you with a marriage license in my pocket," he tells her after their reunion in New York. Besides, Kay must announce her engagement to the prosperous Gene Piper in order to save her father from financial ruin. When she does accede to her love for Terry, she does so with an infectious surge of emotion.

In most of her 1930s features, Joan, if she were not playing opposite Gable, needed a restrained, subtle leading man—a Franchot Tone, a Brian Aherne, or a Robert Montgomery—who nonetheless has Joan's number from the outset. Her greatest flair was to convince her public that she had reached the heights of luxury and social acceptance not at the expense of others, but by seizing the tide that, as Shakespeare wrote, leads on to fortune. This instinct for advancement, allied to unstinting application to her work, rendered Joan almost impregnable at the box office.

In *I Live My Life*, Adrian's costumes once again reflect the expansive, often contradictory aspects of Joan's personality. She wears a long black dress with huge white lapels and white cuffs. In another scene, the black is offset by an extravagant variation on the white bow tie so beloved by Adrian. Her ball gown is topped with two massive, almost pharaonic shoulder extensions, and her wedding gown is a fantasy of satin and lace with a white corona. Toward the climax of the film, she tears up the wedding dress, and lays waste to her room, in rapturous rage. Joan is every bit as vehement in such scenes as Jean Arthur or Katharine

~ LEFT
No More Ladies *(1935)*,
*with Robert Montgomery.*

~ OPPOSITE
The Gorgeous Hussy
*(1936), the fifth film in*
*which Joan was directed*
*by Clarence Brown.*

Hepburn. Hints of her future life creep into the dialogue: "I have my eyebrows hand-plucked every Thursday!" declares Kay defiantly. *No More Ladies* (also 1935) begins with a similar scene, as Joan's elegant Marcia tears off her velvet collar and lavish gown in fury in her boudoir, as she realizes that her dinner date will never arrive.

Burdened by period paraphernalia, a galaxy of stars, and political wrangling, *The Gorgeous Hussy* (1936) remains one of Joan's very rare costume movies. She embodies the fictional personality of Margaret O'Neal Eaton, known as Peggy, an innkeeper's daughter in Washington of the 1820s, when Andrew Jackson was gliding with seemingly effortless ease from general to senator and to president. Peggy entrances too many men at the same time—a naval lieutenant, Bow Timberlake (Robert Taylor), to whose zealous courting she

cheerfully submits; the dignified John Randolph (Melvyn Douglas), a Virginian senator at odds with Jackson's vision of the Union; James Stewart's well-meaning but somewhat bumbling "Rowdy" Dow; and Senator John Eaton (Franchot Tone), who becomes her second husband. If one adds to the list the elderly president himself, it's evident that Peggy exerts considerable sway in the nation's capital, in effect serving as an unofficial first lady.

The film unfolds with, in the background, the ominous prospect of secession and civil strife. Joan brings her maturity and experience to bear on her role. Peggy is forthright in her political opinions, and she's a dab hand at accounts. Her face in certain scenes assumes a hard look, as if it were gradually setting in the mold of her later years, recalling Alexander Walker's roguish comment: "Her skin gave her bones a covering as classic as

*Hats, jewelry, and accessories—
all essential parts of Joan's
image during her heyday
at MGM.*

The Last of Mrs. Cheyney
(1937), with Nigel Bruce as
Lord Willie Winton.

the canvas on a prairie wagon: it was made to withstand all weathers."[2] Adrian endows her with accessories by the dozen—buckle belts, broad-brimmed, upswept hats, white puritan-style collars, a fur muff, a black hood for deathbeds, and the ubiquitous bow tie at her throat. Her hair, long and fluent in early scenes, soon yields to the long "fancy curls" of the period.

Peggy acquires the gift of pragmatism, much as Joan herself had done. She survives while her lovers perish. The film marked, perhaps, the apogee of Joan's career in Hollywood—a vehicle created for her star appeal, with so many famous names circling her in homage (although Lionel Barrymore doesn't so much steal as devour the picture), and a final scene that reflected the short-lived bliss of her private life at that juncture in 1936, as Franchot Tone squires her off to Spain...

Although Joan welcomed *Love on the Run* (1936) as her "first real comedy in ages,"[3] and although she could enjoy being pursued by both Clark Gable and Franchot Tone, this film today is one of her least impressive. By now she could slip without hesitation into the guise of an American heiress, and she relishes the chance to abandon her wedding plans and run off with Gable (as a naive if forceful newshound). The erratic plot takes them to France, where a dastardly baron and his wife are in pursuit of secret documents. They all end up in Fontainebleau palace, where a deranged caretaker, played by the always engaging Donald Meek, presides over his royal domain.

Joan may still refer to herself as a "girl," but she is beginning to deal with the kind of comment that only a woman in her thirties can. Barney Pells (Tone), Gable's rival journalist, tells her, "You've

got a very pretty profile. It fits into your neck like it was made by a mechanic." To which she replies, with a jaw more firmly set than ever before, "Lovely thought, Barney."

In the film's second sequence, Adrian provides Joan with yet another wedding gown, diaphanous, with slender white hoops around both bodice and sleeves. He maintains the sheer, white look throughout *Love on the Run*, with a long, sequined gown, and then an all-white suit with ribbed shoulder seams and a white hat rimmed in dark blue or black.

In late 1936, Joan responded to the direction of Dorothy Arzner, the only woman to have enjoyed the director's chair during the golden age of Hollywood. Arzner worked uncredited on *The Last of Mrs. Cheyney* (1937), at first with Richard Boleslawski (who died of water poisoning a few

days into the shoot) and then George Fitzmaurice as director. But a few months later she took the helm for one of Joan's most intriguing and richly nuanced films, *The Bride Wore Red* (1937). Both pictures stemmed from stage plays, the first from an enjoyable melodrama by Frederick Lonsdale, the great rival and contemporary of Somerset Maugham, the second from a romantic comedy by the Hungarian playwright Ferenc Molnár.

The trenchant wit of Samson Raphaelson can be detected at certain moments in the screenplay for *The Last of Mrs. Cheyney* which, while charming, oscillates uneasily between frivolity and suspense. Joan's role as Fay Cheyney thrives on ambiguity, as would her character in *A Woman's Face* four years later. She loathes the dark side of her personality, the jewel thief surrounded by seedy partners, and sparkles in her everyday incarnation—as the cynosure of an aristocratic house party in Britain, where three lords vie for her hand. As her partner in crime, Charles (William Powell), comments, she is caught "between a string of pearls and a string of peers." Fay herself hears from the Duchess of Ebley that she is "a respectable woman with the soul of an adventuress," and when finally unmasked as a larcenist, Joan quips: "Actually, I'm an adventuress with the soul of a respectable woman."

With each passing film, Joan appears more relaxed, more assured. Accustomed to receiving compliments, she radiates the self-confidence of a woman widely and intimately desired by the men around her. Her acting technique accommodates the subtle touch, be it a sidelong glance of derision as she plays the piano, or a sly lowering of her false eyelashes, like sun-blinds closing. She sweeps into a salon, shoulders at full stretch, hair drawn back to

reveal as much as possible of that gorgeous face and neck. She enunciates and articulates well, giving breath to her diphthongs and stress to her consonants. Joan is containment personified, succumbing rarely if ever to tears, and even less so to schmaltz. In short, her cordiality perplexes rivals and admirers alike. All this attests to her indefatigable discipline and professional commitment, at a juncture when, by her own admission, she was "having personal problems and...let them get in the way."[4] Discreet as always, she does not specify the nature of her private anguish, but it may well have been her continuing inability to sustain a pregnancy. Joan believed that had she performed at full strength in *The Last of Mrs. Cheyney*, she would have earned an Academy Award nomination.[5]

*The Bride Wore Red* marks the transition for Joan between youth and maturity. As a cabaret girl

~ ABOVE *The Bride Wore Red (1937), Joan in her peasant dress, trying not to break down as she deceives Robert Young.*

~ OPPOSITE *The Bride Wore Red (1937), photo by George Hurrell.*

from Trieste, she can flirt like a girl, and rinse her face in a mountain stream with a zest and vigor unbecoming to a lady. She can switch at the drop of a gypsy hat from the bitterness and vulgarity of a working girl to the calculating hauteur of a pseudo-aristocrat. She gives the character of Anni, however, a sultry verve more associated with Garbo, a likeness emphasized by her long, straight hair drawn away from the forehead and by the endless eyebrows, penciled in deep crescents on her evenly lit face. (George Folsey had photographed five of Joan's films already, and would become her favorite cinematographer.)

The film turns on the nature of identity. Is a waiter intrinsically different than an aristocrat? Can a postman in the Swiss (or is it the Austrian?) Alps really be none other than Franchot Tone? Given a two-week vacation in the mountains by a

susceptible count, who sees her singing in a decrepit waterfront café, Anni enjoys the high life so much that she runs up huge bills and must invent ever more preposterous excuses to prolong her stay—and the illusion of wealth and social standing. Tone, with his oak-aged voice and guileless features, waits humbly in the background until she finally accepts him, discarding her austere Garboesque cloak to reveal her peasant dress.

Gowns play a key role in *The Bride Wore Red*. Anni is introduced with gardenias at her shoulder strap. Singing "Who Wants Love?" her face is gauzed with cigarette smoke. Once endowed by the count, though, she demands a scarlet evening dress, and adopts a blue coat with massive fur lapels, leaving her head free to float like a swan's above the tumult. At a dinner in the mountain resort, she wears a gossamer dream of a dress,

*Photo by Clarence Sinclair Bull, 1933.*

Mannequin *(1937), with Spencer Tracy. This was one of three films in which Joan responded to the direction of Frank Borzage.*

with a fine lace scarf over her head, and a fan in hand, to balance the effect of her décolletage. On another occasion, she appears in a cream satin evening gown with great shoulder buttresses composed of what look like insubstantial whorls of material. She orders a folkloric outfit, with puffed shoulders, naturally, and dons it with her hair encircled with alpine flowers. Adrian excels himself with the title gown, a dress that hugs Joan's contours as never before, glittering as though with a mermaid's scales. This extraordinary creation, with its matching cape, weighed thirty pounds, and was made with two million bugle beads (as opposed to sequins). Once beaded, the material was hand-crocheted on crepe romaine.[6] Rehearsals were done with a muslin copy of the gown, as Dorothy Arzner wanted each scene completed in a single take.

## BOX-OFFICE POISON?

*"It's only because of my fans that I'm not still living in a one-room apartment behind a Kansas City wash house."*[7]

If in *The Bride Wore Red* Joan played a Cinderella who stays beyond midnight, the analogy could apply to her career at this juncture. The film flopped at the box office, and exhibitors at last dared to round on Joan. *Life* magazine may have proclaimed her "First Queen of the Movies" in 1937, but early the following year Harry Brandt, president of the Independent Theater Owners of America, wrote in the association's trade paper that Joan's films, along with those featuring Marlene Dietrich, Fred Astaire, Greta Garbo, and Katharine Hepburn, were no longer delivering the goods. She was "box-office poison," he claimed, a term designed and destined to haunt Joan. The press department at MGM

promptly issued a release stating that Joan had just received her 900,000th fan letter. Nor was the claim mere hyperbole. During the six-week period between Thanksgiving and the end of each year, Joan would "personally type, sign and mail ten thousand letters."[8]

Although MGM's response to Harry Brandt's jibe was to sign a fresh contract with Joan, offering her up to $330,000 per annum for the next five years, perhaps some damage had been done. A turning point had been reached in the career of Hollywood's most consistently successful star. For more than nine months (between late October 1937 and late August 1938) Joan deserted the studio floor, an interval without precedent since her arrival in Los Angeles a dozen years earlier. On July 20, 1938, she and Franchot Tone announced their divorce. Once again, Joan's marriage had

lasted but four years. Franchot, after so long in the shadow of his wife, would never become a major star. He lacked assertiveness, and his frustration led him to react with violence against Joan, for she would arrive on set with makeup concealing bruises. "I didn't realize that his insecurities and dissatisfactions ran so deeply," she conceded. "His sex life diminished considerably, which didn't help matters, and there finally came a time when we only had things to argue about, not to talk about, and after hundreds of running arguments and a few physical rows we decided to call it quits."[9] Always gracious and tactful in failure, Joan refused to condemn any of her husbands or lovers. When Franchot fell desperately ill with cancer in his early sixties, Joan helped with the medical bills, and even spent a week with him in his holiday haunt at Lake Muskoka in Ontario.

*Mannequin* (1937) features Joan as Jessie Cassidy, a victim of the Depression who finds herself attracted to two vastly different men. Frank Borzage's direction brings to the hackneyed plot an ominous bass line, a bitter dialectic involving the self-made magnate John L. Hennessey (Spencer Tracy) on the one side, and the impoverished Cassidy family on the other. In a brilliant opening sequence, Jessie comes home from another day at the factory and trudges up three flights of stairs to the dingy apartment on Hester Street in New York that she shares with her parents and brother. Cinematographer George Folsey used a 75-foot boom so the camera could follow her on this symbolic climb, emphasizing the somber décor and the mechanical rhythm of Jessie's movements. It's a shot that might almost belong to the world of G. W. Pabst, and that evokes the slum conditions described in the novels of Charles Dickens or Theodore Dreiser.

Once again, Adrian clads Joan in a black dress with a startlingly white, Puritan-style collar. Her hair is long and voluminous—no hairpiece here as she brushes it all back in a cascade, counting each stroke as she talks to her husband, Eddie. Later, as she models new gowns at a fashion house on Park Avenue, she runs through Adrian's gamut of styles (as she did, of course, in *Our Blushing Brides*), using each new outfit as an excuse for flirting with Hennessey, who has come to see the show.

If by now it was a cliché to find Joan caught between good and evil, between poverty and wealth, between the boyfriend of her youth and the mature man of her dreams, *Mannequin* renders the situation more ambivalent. Tracy's Hennessey may be infinitely courteous—even when threatened by a strike in his shipyards—but he is accustomed to getting what he wants, and evinces a ruthless streak at odds with Jessie's ideal. Eddie, played by

~ *A sturdy Joan saving Margaret Sullavan from committing suicide amid the flames in* The Shining Hour *(1938).*

the smarmy, snarling Alan Curtis, embodies the opportunism that Roosevelt's New Deal sometimes engendered, despite its good intentions. Eddie urges Jessie to divorce him, marry Hennessey, and then divorce *him* in order to extract a ton of alimony. Jessie's younger brother shares this cynical approach to life, exploiting government relief and sneering at his sister's orthodox work ethic.

Joan seems to exert no effort in playing the part of Jessie. After all, by her admission, "for centuries I was the girl from the wrong side of the tracks who crossed over."[10] Hervé Dumont, in his magisterial study of Borzage's work[11], asserts that *Mannequin* is Joan's "most honest" film, quoting the French critic Christian Viviani's reference to her "inner suffering, her vulnerability, the anguish of a malnourished teenager."[12] Yet it was not a wholly satisfactory film, with its abrasive dialogue alternating with scenes of mawkish sentimentality.

During production, Spencer Tracy did not behave well toward Joan, despite their initial attraction to each other. "We even whooped it up a little bit off the set," said Joan, "but he turned out to be a real bastard. When he drank he was mean, and he drank all through production."[13] Tracy would chew on garlic, and step on her toes during a love scene.

Borzage's *The Shining Hour* (1938) restored Joan to the moneyed classes, even if she is but a nightclub dancer who marries into a wealthy Wisconsin family. She's confronted by a malicious sister-in-law, Hannah, who deploys one ruse after another to undermine the marriage. The screenplay, in part written by the droll Ogden Nash, focuses on the smugness and pettiness of the siblings in the Linden family. Joan's character, Olivia, is a mass of conflicting shades and colors. She accepts life as it comes, her smile starting hesitantly and then switching on like a light. She weathers a

~ The Women *(1939), with Rosalind Russell.*

constant barrage of criticism from Hannah, and continues to wear dramatic clothes to her own liking—a long, gleaming engagement gown, with a deep, if slender-cut V-neck; a cocktail dress with shoulders so square-cut that they form almost a yoke; or a check-print waistcoat over a billowing white dress with insubstantial puff shoulders. Yet when the crisis arises, she behaves like a true heroine, rescuing Margaret Sullavan's Judy from a burning house, even though Judy has tried to sacrifice herself so that her husband, David (Robert Young), manifestly in love with Olivia, can remarry.

With each passing film there is more resolve in Joan's features. When Olivia decides to quit the Wisconsin estate at the close of the film, she tells her brother-in-law, "She rides fastest who rides alone," adding, "I look like a lady—sometimes."

Two films shot during the closing year of the decade encapsulate the changing look and fortunes of Joan Crawford. In *The Women,* Joan had to settle for almost a supporting role (even though she fought for it)—all the more galling because her old rival Norma Shearer took the lead. *Strange Cargo* marked the end of her onscreen partnership with Clark Gable (if not the end of their relationship in private life), and presented her shorn of opulence. This film, her third under the direction of Frank Borzage, would prove a harbinger of the kind of unvarnished, hard-edged roles Joan would accept in the postwar years.

George Cukor could hardly have failed with his screen adaptation of Clare Boothe's play, *The Women,* especially as Anita Loos brought additional acerbity to the script after Scott Fitzgerald's draft had been virtually dismissed. The contrast between the four main "women" is astringent: Norma Shearer as Mary Haines, always cheerful and brisk, unaware of her husband's affair with Joan's Crystal

The Women *(1939)*,
*photo by Laszlo Willinger.*

The Women *(1939)*,
*with Norma Shearer
and Rosalind Russell.*

Allen; Rosalind Russell as the bitchy Sylvia; Paulette Goddard as Miriam; and Joan Fontaine as Peggy. If the bevy of hairdos, hats, brooches, and other accessories tends to outshine the dialogue, the film does press home the distinctions between Shearer and Crawford. Norma is so proper, so bourgeois; Joan is indefatigably working-class. Norma is the victim who personifies grace under pressure; Joan determines to get revenge even as she fights back tears of humiliation.

Joan clearly relishes her role in *The Women*. In what Carlos Clarens called "an epochal performance as the hard-as-nails Other Woman,"[14] she gives savage bite to lines such as, "He almost stood me up for his *wife*." After eighteen months of marriage, Crystal relaxes in a foam bath, smoking and phoning yet another new lover. She also gets the last word in her lethal confrontation with Shearer, her

brazen vulgarity winning the day. Crystal Allen was, said Joan, "the epitome of the hard-headed, hard-hearted gold-digger on the big make, a really nasty woman who made the audience want to hiss."[15]

*Strange Cargo* (1940) was the antithesis of Cukor's boulevard comedy. For the first time in her career, glamour was not a prerequisite for Joan. For *The Women*, she recalled bitterly, "I'd had a $40,000 wardrobe. For *Strange Cargo* I had three dresses, worth less than forty dollars altogether."[16] Her character had survived an ordeal by fire in *The Shining Hour*, but in *Strange Cargo* she had to struggle against thirst, storms, and the perils of a South American jungle. As in *Rain*, she plays a hard-bitten prostitute in a tropical backwater. She's expelled from the island "deep in the Guianas" (actually Devil's Island, but MGM did not wish to offend the French government) after being caught

with Clark Gable's intractable and lascivious convict. The film quickens after Gable escapes from the penal colony with some other prisoners, each of whom emerges as an intriguing personality, each seeking some kind of redemption, with their fears and aspirations articulated by the mysterious Cambreau. Ian Hunter's spare, restrained performance as Cambreau makes this religious figure much more credible than Walter Huston's preacher in *Rain*—one of the reasons *Strange Cargo* belongs among Joan's best films, and *Rain* among her least successful.

Although she campaigned successfully to have her name above Gable's in the credits, Joan in her heart must have known that unless she adapted her personality, she could no longer play the bright young star at MGM. So, as always, she did adapt. As she plunges through the jungle with Gable, she is reduced to a muddy wreck, stripped of makeup and sophistication. By the light of a campfire she does make a token attempt to reach for her lipstick, and to comb her hair using the lid of a can as a mirror. Aboard the boat that takes the prisoners to the mainland by night, she becomes an object of desire, flashing a generous swathe of thigh, with the moonlight reflected on her perspiring neckline.

"Clark and I did our best work together in *Strange Cargo*," she reminisced. "Now we knew each other as mature persons and the chemistry was still there and it added to the fire."[17] Gable had completed filming on *Gone with the Wind*, and although the epic was in the final editing stage when *Strange Cargo* was shot, there was no doubt in Hollywood that Gable had reached a new peak in his career. What Hervé Dumont has called "the passionate violence" of the exchanges between Joan and Gable had to be tempered in

~ During the Depression years, Joan exuded a confidence that especially delighted her fans. Photo at left by Laszlo Willinger, 1939.

the face of pressure from the Legion of Decency, which branded the film an "amalgam of religion and licentiousness."[18] As the producer Joseph L. Mankiewicz exclaimed in 1978: "Christ, you couldn't even indicate that Clark Gable screwed Joan Crawford in their trek through the jungle on the way to the beach!"[19]

Her fans dreaded the aging of Joan Crawford. They kept abreast of every detail of her private existence. As Mankiewicz noted, "She woke up like a movie star, she went to the john like a movie star. She had a special outfit for answering fan mail. She put on another outfit to have lunch."[20] She slept in white pajamas or short nightgowns. She took four showers or more each day. She loved Coty's Jungle Gardenia perfume, and her favorite color was green. Her myriad shoes were size four. Her hair was "very fine," by her own admission.[21] "Fans have made me what I am today," she told journalists.[22]

As World War II gathered momentum in Europe, Joan sensed that her life and career were being wracked by change. In November 1939 she suffered from a depression so acute that she missed three full days of shooting on *Strange Cargo*, a lapse unprecedented in her career. This occurred only a few weeks after she had adopted Christina, although an announcement of the adoption would not be made until 1940. On the surface this event seemed a moment of joy, but it also marked Joan's final acknowledgment that she could not bear a child herself. She sought relief from her private anguish by accepting her public image. "Did you know there were twenty-five thousand baby girls christened with the name Joan this year?" she wrote in a letter a few months later. "Half were named after me, and the others were named for Joan of Arc. Isn't that wonderful?"[23]

Joan was gradually becoming Crawford.

~ OPPOSITE  *Photo by George Hurrell, 1935.*

~ ABOVE  *Photo by George Hurrell, 1936.*

~ ABOVE *Joan in a supercilious mood. Photo by George Hurrell, 1937.*

~ OPPOSITE *1935.*

FOUR

# THE RELUCTANT DOMINA

(1940 TO 1970)

## "Crawford looking about as wobbly as the Statue of Liberty..."

MOLLY HASKELL

~

OAN CRAWFORD HAD MAN-
aged the transition from silence to
sound with consummate aplomb.
The World War II years, however, proved a larger
barrier that she negotiated only at the expense of a
radical change in her screen image. Between 1940
and 1945 she adopted two children, Christina and
Phillip (although his name was later changed to
Christopher). She married for a third time, to the
actor Phillip Terry. Her seventeen-year commitment to MGM came to a sad conclusion, with
Crawford paying the studio $50,000 in lieu of the
one film still due under her contract. She moved to
Warner Brothers and made a triumphant debut at
the Burbank studio with *Mildred Pierce* (1945).

Last but not least, her emblematic couturier,
Gilbert Adrian, also left MGM and would not dress
Crawford again in a motion picture. Looking back,

she said: "If I can put my finger on the time of
change, I think that when World War II ended, the
fun aspects went out of American movie-making,
and that sense of fun never returned."[2]

As the nation emerged from the Depression,
only to face the prospect of a Europe convulsed by
war, younger talents were vying for star billing at
MGM, including Lana Turner, Hedy Lamarr, and
Greer Garson. Crawford had to adapt to these circumstances, and by the time peace had been
achieved in 1945, she had reemerged as Mildred
Pierce, and from that point on she would appear
more severe, more judgmental, a dominatrix in
waiting. It required courage, for had she retired on
the cusp of the war years, her reputation as an
actress might have grown over time.

*Susan and God* (1940) is a transitional film in
Crawford's career. A winsome concoction about a

~ PREVIOUS *As the carnival girl in* Flamingo Road *(1949).*

~ OPPOSITE *1947.*

reckless New York socialite who returns from Europe a religious convert, the film is saved by Crawford's tart, astringent performance. Fredric March plods along in the role of her alcoholic husband, and Rita Quigley brings their daughter, Blossom, to life. But *Susan and God* betrays its stage origins with a continual flurry of exits and entrances, and even George Cukor's urbane direction cannot ignite the drama.

Crawford's gowns (by Adrian, still) are more flamboyant than ever. Her most memorable dress hangs by a cord around her neck, the broad vertical stripes emphasizing her back and shoulders, and a wide belt in the same material completes the assertive image. A white day dress with short sleeves and, again, vigorous stripes is topped with a Quaker-style collar and matching belt. Her final outfit, full-length, boasts tendrils of white material tied at her neck, hips, and sleeves.

Crawford remarked that her belief in Christian Science stemmed from her filming of *Susan and God*, and her reading and learning about the faith. "I firmly believe the body can cure its ailments through faith instead of medication or surgery."[3]

If *Susan and God* seemed like some vestige of the 1930s, *A Woman's Face* (1941) belongs indisputably to Crawford's new era. Ingrid Bergman had already made an impact in the first screen version of Francis de Croisset's play about a woman, scarred in an accident, who exacts revenge on society by becoming a blackmailer. Louis B. Mayer acquired the remake rights at Crawford's urging, but felt that Garbo would be better equipped to take the role of Anna Holm. He offered the Swedish actress a choice of projects: *A Woman's Face* or *Two-Faced Woman*. Fortunately for Crawford, Garbo chose the latter. Mayer remained

dubious, even aghast, at the prospect of his most prolific star playing such an unsympathetic part.

Cukor again took the helm. He found Crawford "very easy to work with, very sensitive," and said he felt that she realized "that the part was 'twisted.' Right before every scene, in fact, she'd try to 'twist' herself mentally."[4] Rehearsals were intense. Crawford remembered the "hours of drilling, with camera and lights lined up for the opening sequence in the courtroom, *then* Mr. Cukor had me recite the multiplication table by twos until all emotion was drained and I was totally exhausted, my voice dwindled to a tired monotone."[5]

The revelation of Anna's scarred face has a shock impact similar to the murder of Janet Leigh in *Psycho*. Adrian creates a disguise in the form of a hat with a length of crepe hanging down the right side of her face and upper body, while cinematographer Robert Planck highlights the left

cheekbone and her eyes and mouth. Dark hair and somber clothes are the order of the day. Crawford's beauty is breathtakingly classical, evoking Nefertiti with its impeccable profile.

Not since *Letty Lynton* (1932) had Crawford played a woman so intent on vengeance. Ingrid Bergman may have been more derisive, more gloating in the first half hour of the Swedish original, but Crawford gives Anna Holm an underlying rancor appropriate to the character as a whole. Bitter, and envious of other women's beauty, Anna has by her own admission taken refuge in both liquor and music. She has become a predator, using stolen letters to blackmail the foolish and the indiscreet. Conrad Veidt plays Torsten Barring, who draws Anna into his evil sphere. "We are both proud, both wretched," he smirks. Crawford can project guile, but not with such control as Veidt, whose suave malevolence belongs unmistakably to the

~ ABOVE **When Ladies Meet** *(1941), with Spring Byington.*

~ OPPOSITE **When Ladies Meet** *(1941), with Robert Taylor.*

fledgling world of film noir. Like James Mason or Eric Portman, he is sinister and diabolically intelligent. Once a surgeon has removed her scar, Anna finds the prospect of a new life conflicting with the temptation to return to her criminal ways. In a climax set in northern Sweden (with sets immaculately dressed by Cedric Gibbons), she at last rejects her past, and escapes into the light of a relationship with Melvyn Douglas's dry but watchful surgeon.

Right to the end, Adrian insists on black—a dark mink fur coat with snug-fitting fur cap to match. Six months after the film appeared, Adrian left MGM. Gowns, for both him and Crawford, had lost their social allure. No longer could Crawford represent the shopgirl's fantasy. Circumstances obliged her to survive by her wits and tenacity and with what Otto Friedrich has called her "animal ambition."[6] Clothes could not conceal the signs of

age forever. Instead, her acting skills, like her fabled cheekbones, became increasingly prominent. Even Cecilia Ager admired "the mastered casualness" of her English diction.[7]

Adrian would dress Crawford on one final occasion, however. *When Ladies Meet* (1941), may have been merely a post-Wildean comedy of manners, but it signified more in Crawford's twilight years at MGM. For the first time, she was faced with a female rival endowed with glamour and charisma. Greer Garson was almost exactly the same age as Crawford, but she appeared in her first Hollywood film (*Goodbye Mr. Chips*) only in 1939. British by birth, and with a wealth of stage experience to her credit, Garson steals every scene in which she features in *When Ladies Meet*. As the poised, long-suffering wife of Herbert Marshall's philandering publisher, she confronts Crawford

who is cast yet again as the "other woman." Garson has all the best lines, and Adrian's figure-hugging dresses give her a desirable dimension that must have irritated Crawford, whose own performance is adequate if not inspired. MGM must have felt that Crawford by now needed some support in the sexual stakes. Although she may win handsome Robert Taylor in the final shot, her part is essentially that of a frumpish authoress, at odds with Crawford's innate elegance. For an intimate dinner with her publisher- lover, Adrian at least blesses her with one magnificent outfit—close-fitting, sheer white, and with a finely pleated skirt.

Clearly, her time at MGM was ebbing to a close. In 1942, she honored her contract with *Reunion in France*—but she seemed be performing on automatic pilot. The studio lent her to Columbia to replace Gable's beloved wife Carole Lombard in

*They All Kissed the Bride*. Crawford, who had comforted Gable after Lombard's death in a plane crash, donated her salary of $128,000 for the comedy to the Red Cross, whose representatives had located Lombard's body in the mountains.

Diverted perhaps by her marriage to Phillip Terry, a decision that illustrated the triumph of hope over experience, she threw herself into the mood of the times, aiding the war effort whenever and wherever she could. She closed part of her spacious home in Brentwood, and because of the fuel shortage, she opted for a motorbike with sidecar (for the children). She and Terry cultivated a vegetable garden on the front lawn. Even before Pearl Harbor, Crawford served as chairwoman of a charity raising funds for children orphaned in the London blitz. Sunday was an "open day" at her home, with visitors paying a few cents to see the

*Joan with her third husband, Phillip Terry, 1943.*

Reunion in France *(1942), an uneasy and unconvincing screen partnership with John Wayne.*

"Victory Garden" and purchase autographed pictures of the actress—all for a good cause.[8]

Terry's role as her husband confirmed Crawford's need for a partner who would play liege man to her queen. Like Franchot Tone, Terry radiated calm and adoration for his wife. Crawford was proud of his academic credentials; he had graduated from Stanford and had studied at the Royal Academy of Dramatic Arts in London. John Wayne, her unlikely costar in *Reunion in France*, remarked: "I knew what kind of a marriage it was going to be when I saw her walk on the set. First came Joan, then her secretary, then her makeup man, then her wardrobe woman, finally Phil Terry, carrying the dog."[9] If he had a fault, it lay in his fondness for cocktails; Crawford had not been a regular drinker before meeting Terry, and from then on she would rely on liquor to nourish her self-confidence.

*Reunion in France*, released barely a month before the similar but infinitely superior *Casablanca*, is justly forgotten today. John Wayne is appallingly incongruous and folksy as the Yankee flyer stranded in Nazi-occupied Paris. Crawford might seem even more out of place as the wife of a Nazi sympathizer, but she extracts maximum effect from her lines, often sardonic and insinuating at the expense of traitors and cowards alike ("A severe wound, I hope," she tells an injured Nazi officer). Dressed in some appalling gowns and furs by Irene, she dwells in an ivory tower of luxury. Her perfidious husband compares her maliciously to "La France," as being "spoiled, selfish, incurably romantic."

Her final film at MGM, *Above Suspicion* (1943), may have been more frivolous in tone, but its production proved much more enjoyable an experience for everyone involved. It attracted large

∽ ABOVE *With David Brian, Vincent Sherman, and Steve Cochran, 1950.*

∽ OPPOSITE *At home in Brentwood, with her dachshunds.*

audiences, enabling Crawford to depart from MGM with head held high. The picturesque look of the film suggested that as far as the war was concerned, much of Hollywood still dwelt in a fantasy land. Conflating Austria and Germany in a series of Ruritanian miniatures and mountain backdrops, the production offers the amiable Fred MacMurray as an unlikely Rhodes scholar who marries a fellow Oxford undergraduate, Frances (Crawford), and is then inveigled into hunting down the plans for a secret German weapon in the depths of the Third Reich. Crawford reacts as instructed, either beaming with delight or directing a somber gaze at treacherous Nazis like Basil Rathbone's Sig von Aschenhausen. Toward the climax of the film, her hair is transformed from a brunette ponytail by a vivid blond rinse, complete with a center part and tightly coiled braids at the side of her face; only a

dirndl seems lacking from her folkloric disguise as she tries to escape from the enemy. She revels in lines that mock the Nazis: Under torture she exclaims, "I've already told you I don't know—and if you bring in Goering, Goebbels, and Himmler my answer will still be the same!"

In June 1943, Joan Crawford left MGM, after seventeen years and sixty films. It remains unclear whether she was eased out by Louis B. Mayer or if Crawford herself decided that she must have a change, even if at the press conference announcing her departure Mayer declared her to be "yet another favorite daughter."[10] In her memoirs, Crawford explained, "Mr. Mayer didn't want me to leave. But he realized how unhappy I'd become, and at last, reluctantly, he persuaded Nick Schenck [head of Loew's Inc., which controlled MGM] to give me my release." Even though the studio held

~ Mildred Pierce *(1945), the fire of repressed passion* . . .

no farewell party in her honor, and even though she carried her own belongings out to the trunk of her car with no one to help her, Crawford never criticized Mayer. He was, she told John Kobal in the closing years of her life, "my father confessor: the best friend I ever had."[11]

## MILDRED AND THE
## MYSTIQUE OF GLAMOUR

*"From* Mildred Pierce *onwards, a show of innocence was impossible. Her portrayals could no longer be complementary to men, they were competitive with men. She sought to destroy them, not entice them."*
—BOB THOMAS[12]

Two men revived Crawford's career at this juncture. One was the producer Jerry Wald, and the other Lew Wasserman, the MCA agent who took her under his wing, as he did Bette Davis, Betty Grable, Errol Flynn, Paulette Goddard, James Stewart, Alfred Hitchcock, and many other Hollywood figures. Just two days after she quit MGM, Crawford signed, with Wasserman in attendance, an exclusive deal with Warner Bros. She agreed to make three films, for a total fee of $500,000.

For two years, Crawford did not star in a studio picture, although in *Hollywood Canteen* (1944), she danced with doughboys to show her commitment to the war effort. She served sandwiches to soldiers and sailors at the Canteen every Monday night, and wrote postcards to their families.[13] Her prolonged absence from the screen was due to her having full authority over choice of script, director, leading men, and crew members. Typical of the offers she refused was *Conflict*, opposite

～ Mildred Pierce *(1945), with Jack Carson as the brash, ardent, and self-confident Wally Fay.*

Humphrey Bogart. "Joan Crawford never dies in her films," she snapped to Jack Warner, and Alexis Smith gladly accepted to fill her shoes.

*Mildred Pierce* (1945) did not come easily to Crawford. Bette Davis was Jack Warner's first choice, but she rejected a role that involved being mother to a seventeen-year-old girl. And Michael Curtiz, the director attached to the project, wanted Barbara Stanwyck for the part. Both were "hot," Curtiz in the wake of *Casablanca*, and Stanwyck fresh from her triumph in *Double Indemnity*. But Crawford's principal ally at Warner Bros. was Jerry Wald, who had started his career as a screenwriter and became one of the studio's stalwart producers, with pictures like John Huston's *Across the Pacific* and Delmer Daves's *Destination Tokyo* to his credit. Wald persuaded both Curtiz and Warner to select Crawford for the role of the hard-working former

housewife who becomes a successful restaurateur and is exploited by her lovers and her thankless daughter. Ranald MacDougall was assigned to write a screenplay from James M. Cain's bestseller, with Warners's new star in mind.

"Curtiz had the great good sense," she recalled, "to let Mildred grow beyond the original script."[14] The character developed into what she termed "a composite of the roles I'd always played—and a few elements from my own personality and character."[15]

The contrast between Crawford's final MGM vehicles and her full-blooded debut at Warner Bros. could not have been more startling. Warners was dubbed "Sing-Sing" or "West Point" by its detractors, but the studio's austerity yielded dividends. Films were produced on, or below, budget. Stars and directors adhered to a rigorous schedule.

Crews worked far beyond their regular hours. Producers such as Henry Blanke, Hal Wallis, and Wald himself allowed no film to escape with even a minute of surplus running time.

In this climate, and with World War II raging in Europe and the Far East, Warners prospered with its relentless flow of melodramas, gangster pictures, and war movies. Great technicians gave each Warner production its dark and businesslike look. On *Mildred Pierce*, cinematographer Ernest Haller lit the rain-slicked streets with an ominous glamour; David Weisbart's editing hurried the film from climax to climax; George James Hopkins, who had designed *Casablanca*, brought a sinister geometry to the shadowed beach house where the lovers meet; and the strident chords of Max Steiner's music echoed the anguish and violence of Mildred's predicament. Crawford's costumes were by Milo Anderson, who had churned out the gowns for more than 130 films in fourteen years. He created some cotton frocks for the early sequences of Mildred at home and as a waitress in Glendale. Curtiz rejected them as being "too smart." So Crawford herself went down to Sears Roebuck "and bought the kind of housedresses [she] thought Mildred would wear. Curtiz ranted and raved, 'You and your damned shoulder pads!'"[16] At the wrap party, the star presented her director with a pair of Adrian's oversize shoulder pads. To his credit, Curtiz took the joke. "When I agreed to direct Miss Crawford," he declared to the assembled cast and crew, "I felt she was going to be as stubborn as a mule and I made up my mind to be plenty hard on her. Now that I have learned how sweet she is and how professional and talented she is, I take back even thinking those things about her."[17]

Within the film's running time of 117 minutes, we can see "Joan" mutating into "Crawford." Mildred in the early sequences is a resolute housewife and caring mother, reacting stoically to her husband's running off with a woman down the road. She loses her younger daughter to influenza, and dotes on Veda, the elder. Then, encouraged by her lovers Wally Fay (Jack Carson) and Monte Beragon (Zachary Scott), she launches her own restaurant off Pacific Coast Highway. Soon she is dressing well and driving fine cars. But Veda's egotism knows no bounds: She saps her mother of funds for singing lessons, for clothes, and—in a final act of treachery—for Monte's debts.

As an adaptation of James M. Cain's novel, *Mildred Pierce* remains one of the sublime peaks of film noir. Cain's two other masterpieces, *Double Indemnity* and *The Postman Always Rings Twice*, also rendered life in southern California as a vivid conflict between light and darkness. But while *Mildred Pierce* the novel starts in a relatively benign mood, and builds to a climax of relentless, almost sickening intensity, MacDougall's script leaps back and forth in time, plunging the audience from the start into a chiaroscuro world of panic and passion and concluding with murder most foul. Only Crawford could appear as Mildred mysteriously does, drifting by night across a pier glistening with rain, clad in a lustrous fur coat and matching cap, earrings gleaming, makeup impeccable despite the hour and the pressure, ready to commit suicide until stopped by a passing cop.

The role inspired Crawford to find new resources, fresh subtleties of technique that make of Mildred one of the greatest of all Hollywood screen characters. Her lips retain a sensual fullness even when she sets her jaw in reaction to bad news. She is courageous in her solitude, dignified in the face of scorn. Certain lines in the novel, such as "the glittering tears made her eyes look hard, cold, and feline," seem almost intended to describe Crawford. Yet Mildred reveals both an innate snobbery (as when she asks Lottie, the black maid, to "announce" each guest at a reception, including

~ *Michael Curtiz brings the Academy Award for* Mildred Pierce *to Crawford's bedside on March 7, 1946.*

Bert, her ex-husband), and a startling ferocity when piqued. "Get out before I kill you!" she threatens Veda, after being slapped to the ground by her sneering daughter. In the original Mac-Dougall screenplay, Mildred thrashes Veda brutally at this juncture, but Crawford felt that it would be out of character. As Alexander Walker commented, "Children in [Crawford's] films are like the pelican's brood—they eat their mother's heart out while she is cherishing them."[18]

This was the performance of a lifetime, and was recognized as such. At last Crawford had escaped from the shadow of Bette Davis as a "serious" actress. James M. Cain sent her a copy of *Mildred Pierce* bound in leather and inscribed: "To Joan Crawford, who brought Mildred to life as I had always hoped she would be and who has my lifelong gratitude."[19] The picture grossed $5.6

million worldwide, four times its budget. The Academy Award for Best Actress crowned her triumph. Suffering from the flu, Crawford listened eagerly to the announcement of the awards radio broadcast from Grauman's Chinese Theater. Michael Curtiz accepted the statuette on her behalf, and then everyone descended on the Crawford home in North Brentwood. "Within minutes," she recalled, "a bevy of people had the place jumping. There was no help, no food; we feasted on effervescence that night, and I was so overheated, the fever broke."[20]

Some months earlier, Crawford had been given a Golden Apple Award by the Hollywood Women's Press Club as "the most cooperative actress of 1945."[21] Beyond the flashing lights, however, her marriage to Phillip Terry had foundered. The couple separated in December 1945 and

~ Humoresque *(1946), Crawford as the neurotic socialite with her protégé, violinist Paul Boray (John Garfield).*

divorced in April 1946, at which point Crawford changed the name of her three-year-old adopted son, from Phillip to Christopher. Terry claimed that his wife had run "her household like a dictator, drawing up a schedule divided into fifteen-minute blocks—and allotting him one hour for sex each afternoon."[22] Other lovers appeared for sporadic flings with Crawford, foremost among them the lawyer Greg Bautzer who, like others before him, was obliged to carry the star's knitting bag and sometimes her poodle. He would even place the napkin in her lap at dinner parties.[23]

*Humoresque* (1946) confirmed the resurrection of Joan Crawford as a blue-chip movie star, and earned $3.4 million globally at the box office. Again produced by Jerry Wald, photographed by light-meister Ernest Haller, and with an eclectic music score by Franz Waxman, who plundered

the classical repertoire, *Humoresque* presented Crawford as Helen Wright, the wealthy muse and patron of a brilliant young violinist, Paul Boray (John Garfield). Shades of the dominatrix appear in Crawford's introductory scene. She hosts a soirée, and, surrounded by sycophantic admirers, teases Boray until he rises to the bait and insults her. "Bad manners, Mr. Boray," she smiles, "the infallible sign of talent." Crawford seems taller than she did a decade earlier. Her mouth wears an ill-disguised sneer of disdain and amused self-confidence. Her face looks sculpted, as though liberated from marble. Helen drinks and smokes incessantly. "I'm on a liquid diet," she quips wryly and later when Paul, now her lover, urges her to come home, she says, "Let me alone, Paul, I'm a lost crusade." Her love for him ignites his concert career while destroying her own illusions of

Humoresque *(1946),*
*shoulders back and ready to*
*stride forever into the waves.*

*Ca. 1947.*

grandeur. To the sound of the "Liebestod" from *Tristan and Isolde,* and wearing a sequined black gown, she wades into the moonlit sea in a scene that Cukor would evoke some years later in *A Star Is Born.* Dressed once again by Adrian, she seemed ageless, no longer a young heroine yet still erotically charged, commanding, and ravishing to regard. Clearly, she yearns for her admirers to be stronger than she is, and when they fall short, she must fill the power vacuum. No longer the sparkling innocent, she seemed to acknowledge instinctively the need to assert her authority.

Jack Warner, notoriously ruthless and autocratic with his stars, always responded to box office results, and after *Humoresque* he negotiated a revised contract with Lew Wasserman, paying Crawford $200,000 for each of two films per year for a staggering seven years ahead.

## TORCH SONGS

*"Here was a star to her fingertips: fully conscious of her rather horsy glamour, using her big eyes, her wide gash mouth to splendid effect. Her acting range was limited, but she conveyed an agreeable energy and dash, a hardness and determination, that ensured one's attention for the whole length of a performance. No one could weep like her—hoarse whimpers under fur hats, tears trickling in black mascara rivers down those gaunt cheeks—or smile like her, as though someone had cut her face from ear to ear. Her beauty had a massive quality, baroque and onyx-hard."*

—CHARLES HIGHAM AND JOEL GREENBERG[24]

Joan Crawford would make only four more films during the 1940s, despite the acclaim for *Mildred Pierce.* Advised by her agent Lew Wasserman, she was increasingly selective about her projects. *Possessed* (1947), a far cry from the eponymous film

~ *Crawford as a woman deranged
by love in* Possessed *(1947).*

she had made with Clark Gable sixteen years earlier, continued in the vein of *Mildred Pierce*. Ranald MacDougall again was a guiding hand on the screenplay. From the outset, as Crawford drifts distraught through the city at dawn, the mood is archetypal noir, and Curtis Bernhardt's direction, like Hitchcock's on *Rebecca*, charts the limbo between sanity and derangement. Nurse Louise (Crawford) succumbs to the persistent courting of Raymond Massey's Dean Graham in the wake of his wife's mysterious death. But she also falls under the spell of the devious David Sutton (Van Heflin), and, in a series of flashbacks, she tells psychiatrists about her involvement in the murder of Mrs. Graham, whose daughter accuses her of being responsible for the crime.

For the first time, Crawford plays the role of a desperate woman, and it brought her another Oscar nomination as Best Actress. In the words of Alexander Walker: "A scared Crawford is an awesome sight: her stretched face holds fear the way a sponge holds water."[25] Her lips are drained of color, her eyes bulge above the towering cheekbones, her mouth seems wider than before, the whiteness of her teeth stressed by the dark savagery of her lipstick. She has become a mistress of the baleful glance and the regal walk. Her ankle-strapped shoes became almost a fetish, with open heels and toes that molded to her foot. When producer Jerry Wald objected to the straps, Crawford had them made of plastic that failed to photograph.[26] Women identified with this image of the outsider battling for her place in a somber, macho world. Joan in the late 1920s and early 1930s had gazed up at her costars. The Crawford of postwar years appeared to grow taller and taller with each passing decade. This, too, strengthened the impression of a dominant female surrounded by spavined males.

~ Daisy Kenyon *(1947),*
*Otto Preminger directed*
*Crawford for the first*
*and only time.*

*Daisy Kenyon* (1947), directed by the fiery Austrian expatriate Otto Preminger, did not catch fire, however. Crawford was becoming more demanding on the Warner lot, and when Twentieth Century-Fox asked to borrow the services of his costliest star, Jack Warner did not demur. As a fashion designer living at first in Greenwich Village, Crawford basks in the attentions of Dana Andrews and Henry Fonda. Together they epitomize the men in Crawford's own life—Andrews the lover reluctant to abandon wife and home for his wayward mistress, and Fonda the ex-soldier who plumps for marriage and a romantic life in Cape Cod. Crawford's ever-increasing assertiveness, founded on a profound erotic awareness, explodes in the scene where Andrews tries to undermine her marriage.

The temperature on the *Daisy Kenyon* set had to be 58 degrees, in accordance with the star's contract. After three days, Henry Fonda arrived wearing a raccoon coat. Crawford "was amused, and she presented both of her costars [Fonda and Andrews] with suits of long underwear. The temperature remained the same."[27]

For most of the year 1948, Crawford's preoccupations kept her away from the studio. She adopted twin girls, named Cathy and Cynthia, after their mother had died from kidney failure just a week after giving birth in Tennessee. Her affair with Greg Bautzer became more torrid by the month. As her lifelong friend William Haines once remarked: "To be Joan Crawford's boyfriend, a man must be a combination bull and butler."[28] This made excellent copy for the yellow press, and consolidated Crawford's reputation as a femme fatale. The distinguished critic James Agee wrote of "Joan's desperate beauty and her fine, florid movie personality."[29]

*Flamingo Road* (1949) reunited her with Michael Curtiz, Jerry Wald, Zachary Scott, and composer Max Steiner. Although set somewhere in the South—Missouri or Mississippi—this rancid drama owes much to the tradition of film noir. Lane Bellamy (Crawford) is a carnival dancer who attracts the lascivious attentions of Scott's Fielding Carlisle, the spineless sidekick of Sheriff Titus Semple (Sydney Greenstreet). Semple, envious, has Lane sent to prison on a trumped-up charge. Once released, she grasps eagerly at a job as a waitress (shades of *Mildred Pierce*), and this time catches the eye of David Brian's corrupt business mogul. "You're a very pretty girl," he says with a leer, but although in real life the two would embark on an affair, Crawford is just a tad too old for the part.

Graft dwells beneath every stone in *Flamingo Road,* and the slumberous Greenstreet relishes

every moment of his role as the obese, toadlike sheriff, chuckling at the intrigue that he weaves around his victims. He outflanks Brian's racketeer, pushes Fielding into suicide, and would destroy Lane too, had she not the gumption at last to shoot him. Crawford's costumes were designed by Sheila O'Brien, who would dress the star on seven other features during the 1950s. As Bob Thomas has noted, "Sheila gave Joan dresses so plain they would have seemed drab in a department store, but the designs were enhanced by gorgeous furs and exquisite jewelry, rented or borrowed for the duration of filming."[30]

Crawford's decade ended, as had the 1920s, with a guest cameo, this time in the Doris Day musical *It's a Great Feeling* ("the first comedy I'd done in ages," she recalled, "and I loved every minute of it"[31]). She had outlasted the sexy young

stars from the late 1930s and early 1940s. Even Bette Davis, for so long the queen of the Warner lot, had begun her inevitable decline. As Jack Warner took personal charge of Crawford's career at the studio, she braced herself for change.

Her fans adored her by virtue of her spunky nature, her determination to better herself, and to escape the chains of a conventional relationship. In *The Damned Don't Cry* (1950), they loved her opportunism, as she learns fast how to pursue her own interests and to trade insults and repartee with gangsters and cops alike. As she falls beneath the mortal spell of mobster George Castleman (David Brian), she tells her ineffectual beau (Kent Smith), "He's promised me the world, Marty, and I've gotta have it!" Loosely derived from the unsavory exploits of Bugsy Siegel and his moll, the mysterious socialite Virginia Hill, *The Damned*

*Don't Cry* was directed by Vincent Sherman, with whom Crawford had an affair, and with whom she would make three films in a row.

The old skills sustained her: the exquisite profile, the ineffable elegance of gesture as she turns her face away when a man tries to kiss her. Her body had not betrayed her. Here she eases herself out of a pool in one swift, supple movement. Swimming was a favorite hobby of hers, and a zillion laps had given her deltoids the strength to flaunt her "epaulettes of power,"[32] as Alexander Walker called the shoulder pads she wore in nearly every costume.

The 1950s marked the consecration of Crawford as a gay icon. The image was everything: baleful eyebrows arching in disdain, the mannish, close-cropped coiffure, the predatory smile, and above all the glare of that gaze, suffi-

~ Harriet Craig (1950).

cient to send quailing men to their knees in sub-mission. In *Harriet Craig* (1950), her dominance was complete and her victim was her pliable, easy-going screen husband, Walter (Wendell Corey). Apparently embittered by her inability to bear children, Harriet humiliates family and servants without compunction. She runs her home with ruthless efficiency. Even a cushion out of place provokes her ire. Veteran cinematographer Joseph Walker gives the Craig mansion a crepuscular gloom. Whites are gray, and lamps slung low, enhancing the shadows. Sheila O'Brien dresses Crawford in long gowns that add height and authority to the star as she strides across shrouded rooms or gazes down at the hapless Walter from the grandiose staircase.

Harriet's world collapses about her, despite all her guile and cruelty, and despite her blaming her alcoholic father and her being forced to leave school and start work at the age of fourteen. "You'd never feel safe with anybody until you'd crushed them," says Walter as he deserts her for-ever. Trapped beneath her carapace of loathing, Harriet climbs the stairs to a lonely future. This was the authentic Crawford, at the mercy of her own cast-iron habits, with her vulnerable heart exposed only when it was too late.

Crawford played another aggressive charac-ter, Agatha Reed, in *Goodbye, My Fancy* (1951). This was the third and final occasion on which she was directed by Vincent Sherman. Intent on rekindling a long-vanished relationship with a college presi-dent (Robert Young), her "errant Congresswoman is as aloof and imposing as the Capitol's dome," in the acid words of the *New York Times* reviewer. Fay Kanin's original play presented Agatha as a

～ LEFT
Sudden Fear *(1952), with
scheming husband Jack Palance.*

～ OPPOSITE
Sudden Fear *(1952), Crawford
ready to gun 'em down.*

warmer, more jovial personality, and Katharine Hepburn, or even Rosalind Russell, might have enjoyed playing it more.

Most of the screenplays presented to Crawford now featured female characters of some accomplishment—as befitted her "certain age." In *Sudden Fear* (1952), for example, she was a playwright. Disdaining Warner Bros., she helped to package the project as an independent production at RKO, exacting a 40 percent slice of the gross, as well as a credit as coproducer. Her fee of $240,000 would climb to over $1 million by the time the film had completed its worldwide release.[33] The shoot, however, proved demanding, with a protracted chase sequence through the streets of San Francisco by night, and a glacial relationship with her onscreen lover Jack Palance, who made it plain that he despised her acting abilities.

Crawford helped assemble a first-class crew: director David Miller, who had cut his teeth on B movies and would go on to make the cult Western *Lonely Are the Brave*; composer Elmer Bernstein, whose eerie score was only the second of more than two hundred he would create during his Hollywood career; designer Boris Leven, who had created sets for Fritz Lang and Josef von Sternberg; and above all Charles Lang, the lighting cameraman with a flair for dark interiors and rain-slicked streets. The reward was no fewer than four Oscar nominations, for Crawford, Palance, Lang, and costume designer Sheila O'Brien.

Myra Hudson (Crawford) finds herself seduced and outwitted by a handsome young actor, Lester Blaine (Palance), who persuades her not only to cast him in her new play but to marry him and bequeath him virtually all her money. One feels

that Crawford must have contributed some of her own lines—"I like people who make up their minds and then stick to it, whatever the odds," she tells Blaine. Not for the last time, she plays the woman in jeopardy, her ingenuity and courage saving her in extremis from murder at the hands of Palance and his repellent mistress (Gloria Grahame).

Crawford's look had become more mannish with each passing year. It suited her well in a lightweight vehicle like *This Woman is Dangerous* (1952), about a hard-bitten female gangster who falls for the surgeon who saves her eyesight. As in *The Damned Don't Cry*, she flaunted her furs and jewelry as men would their guns and muscles.

The success of *Sudden Fear* brought Crawford numerous offers, chief among them the role of Karen in *From Here to Eternity*, with billing second only to Montgomery Clift. But she quarreled with Columbia over the screenplay and her wardrobe, and the part went to Deborah Kerr, who would share the most memorable of all 1950s love scenes with Burt Lancaster. Then, her alma mater, MGM, sent her a script entitled *Why Should I Cry?* Crawford responded spontaneously to the part of Jenny Stewart, the Broadway musical star who brooks no criticism, only to fall for her most subtle critic, a blind pianist. She asked for just $125,000 in order to facilitate the production, and accepted payment in eighty-three installments, thus reducing her taxes for the year.[34] At last she could return to one of her favorite pastimes, singing, and she recorded her own voice for one of Jenny's onstage songs, the rest being dubbed by India Adams.

When the film opened in 1953, under the title *Torch Song*, it underlined Crawford's reputation as

a diva. Those who read the movie magazines of the day salivated over the actress's insatiable desire for celebrated lovers, running the gamut from popular studs to closeted homosexuals. The list of her conquests included Rock Hudson, Nicholas Ray, David Miller, Jeff Chandler, Dana Andrews, Brian Donlevy, and Kirk Douglas (who mentions the fling in his autobiography: "At dinner, she was glamorous and very attentive.... We went back to her house. We never got past the foyer.... Afterward, we got dressed. She took me upstairs and proudly showed me the two children—how they were strapped so tightly into their beds, how she diapered them so efficiently. It was so professional, clinical, lacking in warmth, like the sex we just had. I got out fast"[35]). Yul Brynner reputedly sent her a photo of himself with an erection, and leapt into bed with her at the first opportunity.

None of these lovers lasted more than a few weeks or, if he was fortunate, a few months.

*Torch Song* was Crawford's first film in color, and Charles Walters and his team took full advantage of it. The opening scene presents Crawford as an expert dancer, outrageous with orange-blond hair and a wisp of a black chiffon skirt that flaunts her still incomparable legs. Later, she's seen in a saffron yellow, neck-to-foot lounging robe. Then, after singing "Two Faced Woman" with a black wig and blackface makeup, she sees her lover leaving the theater, and tears off her wig in anger, revealing her cropped orange hair beneath!

*Torch Song* reflected splinters of Crawford's own life. She signs letters and photographs for fans, issues brisk instructions to her secretary and cook alike, and checks every detail of costumes being designed for her. Once again, the dialogue

⌐ OPPOSITE
Torch Song *(1953)*.

⌐ RIGHT
Johnny Guitar *(1954), the quintessence
of androgynous authority.*

cuts to the quick. "I don't need anything or any-body. I'm not afraid of being alone," she reads from a script she's running through at home. "Every time you open your mouth," says Tye (Michael Wilding), "you expect to rock the world back on its heels." And Crawford retorts: "I've rocked it a few times!"

Unlike many actors, Crawford never became complacent about her profession. During the eighteen-day shoot of *Torch Song*, for example, she would often stay overnight at the studio, rehearsing her lines alone in her dressing room, wandering around the empty sets, and then snatching a few hours of sleep before being awakened at 5:30 A.M. by her team.[36] She insisted on standing in for herself while her close-ups were being lighted, and she delivered her own offstage lines.[37]

## WEARING THE TROUSERS

*"There is one thing about Crawford you must admire:
her ability to create a myth, a legend about her."*

—STERLING HAYDEN, COSTAR ON *JOHNNY GUITAR*[38]

*Johnny Guitar* emerged from Republic Studios in May 1954, the success of *High Noon* in 1952 and then *Shane* the following year having sustained public interest in the Western genre. Nicholas Ray's brazen extravaganza, cavorting in garish TruColor, might have fared better had it been titled "Vienna and Emma" because the character of Johnny Guitar (Sterling Hayden) is but a pawn in the battle between these two dames, played (one might almost say devoured) by Crawford and Mercedes McCambridge.

Vienna—lonely, fearless, and defiant—defends her right to run a saloon alongside the

projected railroad route through New Mexico, while corrupt town officials, backed by the butch Emma, intend to thwart her. Crawford's role remains the apotheosis of camp in American cinema. She prowls around her domain in boots, saddle-brown britches, and a variety of shirts in every hue imaginable—black, white, canary yellow, vermilion red. Sheila O'Brien's costumes allow Crawford an ultra-ladylike aspect, too. There are freshly creased blouses in gray-blue linen, long, wide-skirted taffeta dresses, and a low-cut, red-currant dress with a deep crimson velvet shawl that makes the star look like some errant Queen of the Night.

Domineering and androgynous, she snarls with hatred at Emma and spurns her former lover, Johnny Guitar. When he displays his sharpshooting skills, Vienna hisses, "Give me that gun!" It's a moment of sheer emasculation, and one senses

that the whip and the paddle are but a heartbeat away. Harry Stradling lights her face so as to emphasize her ice-blue eyes and slash of mouth with her cropped hair in shadow.

Ray directs at fever pitch, with confrontation succeeding confrontation. In a moment of absolute, ravishing kitsch, Emma shoots down Vienna's chandelier so that the whole saloon goes up in flames. Later, a liberated Crawford swims across an icy lake and wades ashore laughing like a young girl. As Martin Scorsese has observed, *"Johnny Guitar* is one of the cinema's great operatic works, pitched from beginning to end in a tone that's convulsive and passionate."[39]

Crawford knew that she had joined the ranks of those female stars—Barbara Stanwyck, Judy Garland, Greta Garbo—who appealed to the gay community. However, just as in *Johnny Guitar* her

~ OPPOSITE *At home at 426 North Bristol Avenue, Brentwood.*

~ ABOVE Female on the Beach *(1955), Crawford as the widow who becomes involved with Jeff Chandler's Drummond Hall.*

feminine softness comes occasionally to light, so in private life she still craved a man whom she could respect, even if she would invariably wear the trousers in domestic (and perhaps sexual) terms. She had become addicted to vodka, drunk straight, to the point that a stranger might think she was sipping a tumbler of water. Her baggage, always considerable, included twenty cases of Smirnoff 100-proof for the six-week *Johnny Guitar* shoot in Sedona.[40] "Vodka relaxed me," she said. "Chased away the butterflies, put a certain distance between me and everybody else."[41] One may ask who introduced the various elements in Crawford's "new look"—the cropped hair, the highlighted eyebrows, the emphatic lipstick? She herself did not so much embrace these changes as consider them indispensable for her status as a star of a certain age. As Bob Thomas has observed,

"She fought against the role of the castrating woman, and yet she was drawn inexorably by the image, both off the screen and on."[42] Competitive to her fingertips, Crawford refused to accept her advancing years, while at the same time she balked at playing the submissive female. She had earned her independence.

New Year's Eve 1954 may well have marked at once the lowest and the highest point of Crawford's emotional life. Relations with her still-young children were tempestuous, to say the least. On December 31, midway through the shoot of *Female on the Beach* (1955), and having elected to stay at the studio overnight while others celebrated, Crawford received a call from friends in Las Vegas. Among them was Alfred Steele, president of Pepsi-Cola, then in the midst of a divorce. Over the next four months, Steele wooed her and they were

married on May 10, 1955, in the Flamingo Hotel in Las Vegas. His command of the business scene impressed her. "I was more in love with Alfred than any other man in my life,"[43] she reflected after he had gone to an early grave. Love can, of course, be measured and compared only with hindsight. Crawford's love for Douglas Fairbanks Jr., Franchot Tone, Clark Gable, Phillip Terry, and Alfred Steele was an intricate blend of circumstance, emotion, and chemistry. Whether for a period of years, months, weeks, or days, Crawford by her own admission felt that bond of passion and understanding that sets "love" apart from the casual affair. A gulf remained between these five men and the convenience lovers who adorned Joan's dinner parties, or squired her to the latest premiere.

Marriage to Steele gave her an inner self-confidence that allowed her to cope with the roles that hove into view at various studios. *Female on the Beach* was produced by Universal, the result of a fling between Crawford and Milton Rackmil, the president of the studio. Crawford could see that the melodramatic story was lacking in credibility. The plot somewhat recalled *Sudden Fear*, with Jeff Chandler as the rugged, muscular neighbor who seduces Crawford's elegant, vulnerable widow.

*Queen Bee* (1955) laid more stress on Crawford's hauteur, bitchiness, and castration potential. A Southern socialite, Eva Phillips, is as used to giving orders to relatives as she is to servants. Her husband complains that she has "the instincts of a head-hunter," and she snaps at her quailing sister-in-law that "Any man's my man, if I want it that way." The joys of sadomasochism quiver just outside the frame, and Eva literally lassoes John Ireland's Judson with the phone cord as she begs out of a dinner engagement in order to spend the night with him. Clad by Jean Louis in a series of gowns worthy

of Adrian, Crawford takes vanity to a fresh extreme, with shoulders, bosom, and back displayed to full if never vulgar advantage.

The character of Milly in *Autumn Leaves* (1956) again encompassed some of Crawford's traits—she is a lonely woman, sustained by a ferocious work ethic. "The future comes so much sooner than it used to," she tells her neighbor and old friend, Liz. The art of living gracefully beguiles her, as does the urge to mother the men around her. When Burt (Cliff Robertson, only thirty at the time) approaches her after a concert at Symphony Hall in Los Angeles, she is uncertain and ill at ease. Terrified by the gulf of age between them, she fends off his advances until, suddenly, she cracks, and they rush down to Mexico to marry. Milly finds herself in emotional and physical jeopardy as details emerge about Burt's past, and the betrayal he suffered at the hands of his father and his first

wife. Crawford's performance admirably suggests the agony that lurks beneath her glacial appearance—hair cut short at the back, ears unshielded like a man's, eyebrows accentuated; and of course the trademark white gloves, and a gardenia on her costume in the concert scene.

In July 1956, Crawford placed her Brentwood home on the market, and prepared to set sail with Steele to England, where she would film *The Story of Esther Costello* (1957) at Shepperton Studios. In the meantime, Steele had bought a duplex apartment at the corner of 70th Street and Fifth Avenue in New York. Crawford found it modest, but set about refurbishing the apartment with the help of William Haines, the renowned decorator and her friend through the decades.

*The Story of Esther Costello*, directed by David Miller, was the only non-American film made by Crawford at that juncture, and the young Jack

Clayton was in charge of production, two years before his breakthrough with *Room at the Top*. The film was based on a novel by Nicholas Monsarrat, a hugely popular author in the UK after the success of *The Cruel Sea*. The role of Margaret Landi seemed tailored for Crawford—a wealthy American, separated from a weak and devious Italian husband (Rossano Brazzi). She takes pity on Esther, a young girl living in poverty in rural Ireland and helplessly blind and deaf after a childhood accident. Her commitment to Esther gives rise to a charity movement that engulfs Margaret and offers tempting wealth to her husband and his cronies.

In moments of joy, Crawford can still smile like a goddess, and a line spoken by the Irish priest in the film must have struck home to her: "You don't seem happy in yourself at all. You've an awful lot to be thankful for." Once more she was

the essence of privilege, a huge apartment in Boston, silk sheets, and a doting maid. Her outfits—sober, restrained, perhaps stressing a bust grown more ample with age—were the work of Julie Harris, a British designer who would win an Oscar for her costumes on *Darling* ten years later. Although *The Story of Esther Costello* succumbs to melodrama and sentimentality in its final third, it provided Crawford with a part that flexed her acting skills while recognizing her "mature" status. Once again, thanks to Robert Krasker's cinematography, she was a clean, well-lighted star.

Three times a divorcée, Crawford at fifty-four became a widow. Alfred Steele died unexpectedly, of heart failure, at the couple's Manhattan apartment on April 19, 1959. "Ours was a romance," she reflected, "that accelerated constantly within marriage rather than, as in so many cases, dwin-

dling down within marriage."[44] As usual, Crawford found consolation and therapy in work. A mere two days after Alfred's death, the directors of Pepsi-Cola voted to give her his place on the board. "I found it very easy. It's lovely to be on a board with nineteen men," she told a British interviewer. "That's exciting!"[45] In years to come she would travel far and wide to promote the Pepsi brand.

*The Best of Everything* (1959) reunited her with Jean Negulesco, who had directed her on *Humoresque*, though he had to persuade her to take a supporting role. "I did it," he admitted with a smile, "by having a scene written for her that was not to be included in the film. But a script-girl told her and spoiled my plans."[46] "The youngsters did all right," she said afterward, "but for some reason or other I'm proud to say I sort of walked off with the film. Perhaps it was the part—I had the balls—

but I think it was a matter of experience, knowing how to make the most of every scene I had."[47]

Amanda Farrow, the senior book editor in *The Best of Everything*, is like a predecessor of Miranda Priestly in *The Devil Wears Prada*—regal, sarcastic, and intimidating. She presides over a publishing company's office and its cat's cradle of soap opera relationships, filled with heartache, exultation, and betrayal. When she lectures Suzy Parker's neophyte actress about love, she hears the retort: "Those who can, do. Those who can't, teach!" Behind her titanium exterior, moreover, she's quivering with insecurity. She resigns to marry a widower from Illinois, and tells one of the junior editors, played by Hope Lange: "He treats me as if he believes I'm the gentlest, softest woman in the world. And maybe, with enough time and tenderness, if it's not too late, maybe I can get to

~ *All smiles at the launch of* What Ever Happened to Baby Jane? *(1962). Bette Davis, Jack Warner, Crawford, and director Robert Aldrich*

believe it myself." These are sentiments she might well have said in real life about her marriage with Alfred Steele.

The final ten years of her screen career brought Crawford only one memorable role, that of Blanche in *What Ever Happened to Baby Jane?* (1962). She divided her time increasingly between guest appearances in TV shows, promoting Pepsi, and working on her memoirs with Jane Kesner Ardmore. She had grown close to Bob Aldrich when he was directing *Autumn Leaves,* and in 1961 he sent her a copy of the gruesome novel *What Ever Happened to Baby Jane?* by Henry Farrell. In November, Crawford visited Bette Davis backstage on Broadway (where she was appearing in *Night of the Iguana*) and told her that she had read *Baby Jane,* and that the book could be an excellent vehicle for both of them. Davis thought immediately of

Hitchcock as director, but he was busy. Negotiations gradually brought the project into focus. Davis was accorded top billing; Crawford did not demur, for the title role, after all, was Bette's.[48] While Davis received a $60,000 fee up front, with 5 percent of the profits to come, Crawford shrewdly bargained for 10 percent of the profits, and only $40,000 as salary. With rentals of more than $4 million in the United States alone, *What Ever Happened to Baby Jane?* cushioned Crawford's final years to a degree she could hardly have anticipated.

It was a grueling shoot, and in many scenes Crawford was humiliated and beaten by her old rival at Warners. She needed all the vodka she could drink. "I really think alcoholism is one of the occupational hazards of being an actor, of being a widow, and of being alone. I'm all three."[49] Yet as Aldrich confirmed in an interview much

～ *With Joseph Cotten on set for* Hush . . . Hush, Sweet Charlotte *(1964). Crawford eventually was replaced in this role by Olivia de Havilland.*

later, "The two stars didn't fight at all. . . . I think it's proper to say that they really detested each other, but they behaved absolutely perfectly. There was never an abrasive word in public, and not once did they try to upstage each other."[50] On October 1, 1962, Crawford was the inaugural guest on *The Tonight Show with Johnny Carson*, and whetted the public's appetite for *Baby Jane*, which opened nationwide later that month.

Crawford's Blanche Hudson, like Gloria Swanson in *Sunset Boulevard*, cherishes the memory of her heyday as a movie star. In 1935, she had script approval on her films, and was earning enough to purchase Rudolph Valentino's former home. But, crippled in a car accident, she must now spend her days in solitary confinement, fed and watered with evident loathing by her sister Jane (Bette Davis). Crawford, given few lines, communicates her fear and anguish through facial expression. Blanche is the victim who, despite her predicament, maintains her decorum and social graces. Crawford works in a lower register than Davis, who can revel in extravagant, grotesque scenes and deliver pungent lines with her trademark malice. *What Ever Happened to Baby Jane?* is a macabre, rancid, and cutrate *Psycho*, and alongside *Johnny Guitar* remains the campiest film in Crawford's career.

It did not, however, rekindle that career. Crawford would feature in just five more films for the big screen, linked by the theme of violence and horror. Two (*Strait-Jacket* and *I Saw What You Did*) were for her friend William Castle. Directors still insisted she flaunt her gams, and in *The Caretakers* and *Berserk!* they look marvelous in tights or fishnet stockings. Somewhere too, deep in her dilated eyes, still lay the bright young thing of *Our Dancing Daughters*.

〜 ABOVE **Berserk!** *(1967), still the best legs in the business.*

〜 OPPOSITE *Warner Brothers publicity shot, 1949.*

Crawford accepted the assignments, however grotesque, because on the one hand she needed the money and on the other she regarded acting as her rationale for living. She urged her admirers not to dwell on those final aberrations and, indeed, why should one when there are more than ten times as many worthier films that she made before World War II? For the last few years of her life, Crawford withdrew from the implacable gaze of the klieg lights. Gradually closing her windows, so to speak, she continued to run her daily life with the discipline that had seen her survive four marriages and forty-five years of stardom.

Joan Crawford died on May 10, 1977, in her bright and tidy Imperial House apartment in New York, bearing the pain of a cancer with extraordinary stoicism. She had forsaken her Alpine cigarettes and her Smirnoff vodka two years earlier. In her final hours she was not alone, but she was not surrounded by children and relatives. Instead she had the company of a housekeeper and, almost symbolically, a female fan. George Cukor spoke eloquently at her memorial service, and in *The New York Times* he wrote: "Somehow I didn't believe that Joan Crawford could ever die.... Come to think of it, as long as celluloid holds together and the word Hollywood means anything to anyone, she never will."[51] She had pursued her happiness through the traditional channels of marriage, motherhood, and career. Stardom, however, was her only loyal companion through the arduous years.

*⁓ A gentler, more relaxed Joan.*

~ On the balcony of her suite at the Beau-Rivage in Lausanne, Switzerland, in 1961.

~ OVERLEAF *The athletic Joan always exulted in the open air.*

# AFTERWORD

*George Cukor*

*This is the text of the eulogy that George Cukor delivered on June 24, 1977, at the Samuel Goldwyn Theater in Los Angeles for the memorial service following Joan Crawford's death.*

I know it sounds off, but somehow I did not believe Joan Crawford could ever die. She was the perfect image of a movie star, and as such largely the creation of her own indomitable will. She had, of course, very remarkable material to work with: a quick native intelligence, tremendous animal vitality, a lovely figure, and above all her face, that extraordinary sculptural construction of lines and planes, finely chiseled like the mask of some classical divinity from fifth-century Greece. It caught the light superbly. You could photograph her from any angle, and the face moved beautifully.

But she was serious with it: serious about improving herself as an actress, serious about her total dedication to onscreen stardom. Though she led a busy life off screen, with husbands, children, and business interests, the career was always central. And she played every role with the same fierce determination, holding back for nothing. In the part of the bitchy, opportunistic girl in *The Women*, she knew perfectly well that she would be surrounded by very formidable competition from the rest of the all-female cast, playing funnier parts and certainly more sympathetic parts, yet she made no appeals for audience sympathy: she was not one of those actresses who have to keep popping out from behind their characters signaling, "Look, it's sweet, lovable me, just pretending to be a tramp." In *A Woman's Face* she played at the outset a disfigured monster of a woman who would not flinch from killing a child, and she did not soften it a bit. Yet in *Susan and God* she found all the comedy in the silly, empty-headed woman who finally, funnily grows to emotional maturity. Whatever she did, she did it wholeheartedly.

Including her love affair with the camera. In the days before zoom lenses and advanced electronics, cameras often had to be mounted on great

~ OPPOSITE *The queen of Hollywood. Any challengers?*

~ *Beside the pool at her home in Brentwood.*

cumbersome cranes, maneuvered by as many as twelve men, and close-ups might well require all this to be pushed from an extreme long shot to within a few inches of an actor's face. Most found it difficult to overcome some understandable nervousness as this juggernaut ground closer and closer. Not Joan Crawford. The nearer the camera, the more tender and yielding she became—her eyes glistened, her lips parted in ecstatic acceptance. The camera saw, I suspect, a side of her that no flesh-and-blood lover ever saw.

But for all that, in private life she was a loving, sentimental creature. A loyal and generous friend, and thoughtful. She forgot nothing: names, dates, obligations. These included Hollywood, the people and institutions who had helped to make and keep her a star. When it was fashionable to rail

against the studio system and the tycoons who had built it, she was always warm in their defense. She spoke of Metro [MGM] as a family, in which she was directed and protected, provided with good stories and just about every male star to play opposite; later she built up a similar relationship with Warners. And through it all, she was constantly herself, unmistakably Joan Crawford.

Katharine Hepburn says that every big star has the talent to irritate. Joan Crawford had that: whether you liked her or did not like her on screen, you could not ignore her existence or deny her quality. I thought Joan Crawford could never die. Come to think of it, as long as celluloid holds together and the word Hollywood means anything to anyone, she never will.

# FILMOGRAPHY

*Excluding television appearances.*
**Silent production.*

### 1925

*Lady of the Night** (JC served as Norma Shearer's double)
*Proud Flesh** (bit part)
*A Slave of Fashion** (a mannequin)
*Pretty Ladies** (Bobby, a showgirl. JC billed for the only time as Lucille LeSueur)
*The Circle** (Young Lady Catherine)
*The Merry Widow** (extra)
*The Midshipman** (extra)
*Old Clothes** (Mary Riley)
*The Only Thing** (party guest)
*Sally, Irene and Mary** (Irene)

### 1926

*Tramp, Tramp, Tramp** (Betty Burton)
*Paris** (cabaret girl)
*The Boob** (Jane, a Prohibition agent)

### 1927

*Winners of the Wilderness** (René Contrecœur)
*The Taxi Dancer** (Joslyn Poe)
*The Understanding Heart** (Monica Dale)
*The Unknown** (Nanon Zanzi)
*Twelve Miles Out** (Jane)
*Spring Fever** (Allie Monte)

### 1928

*West Point** (Betty Channing)
*The Law of the Range** (Betty Dallas)
*Rose-Marie** (Rose-Marie)
*Across to Singapore** (Priscilla Crowninshield)
*Four Walls** (Frieda)
*Our Dancing Daughters** (Diana Medford)
*Dream of Love** (Adrienne Lecouvreur)

### 1929

*The Duke Steps Out** (Susie)
*Tide of Empire* (Josephita Guerrero)
*Our Modern Maidens** (Billie Brown)
*The Hollywood Revue of 1929* (herself)
*Untamed* (Alice "Bingo" Dowling)

### 1930

*Great Day* (uncompleted film)
*Montana Moon* (Joan "Montana" Prescott)
*Our Blushing Brides* (Geraldine March)
*Paid* (Mary Turner)

**1931**

*Dance, Fools, Dance* (Bonnie Jordan, also known as Mary Smith)
*Laughing Sinners* (Ivy "Bunny" Stevens)
*This Modern Age* (Valentine Winters)
*Possessed* (Marian Martin, also known as Mrs. Moreland)

**1932**

*Grand Hotel* (Flaemmchen)
*Letty Lynton* (Letty Lynton)
*Rain* (Sadie Thompson)

**1933**

*Today We Live* (Diana Boyce-Smith)
*Dancing Lady* (Janie "Duchess" Barlow)

**1934**

*Sadie McKee* (Sadie McKee Brennan)
*Chained* (Diane Lovering)
*Forsaking All Others* (Mary Clay)

**1935**

*No More Ladies* (Marcia Townsend Warren)
*I Live My Life* (Kay Bentley, also known as Ann Morrison)

**1936**

*The Gorgeous Hussy* (Margaret O'Neal Eaton)
*Love on the Run* (Sally Parker)

**1937**

*The Last of Mrs. Cheyney* (Fay Cheyney)
*The Bride Wore Red* (Anna "Anni" Pavlovitch)
*Mannequin* (Jessie Cassidy)

**1938**

*The Shining Hour* (Olivia "Maggie" Riley Linden)

**1939**

*The Ice Follies of 1939* (Mary McKay, also known as Sandra Lee)
*The Women* (Crystal Allen)

**1940**

*Strange Cargo* (Julie)
*Susan and God* (Susan Trexel)

**1941**

*A Woman's Face* (Anna Holm, also known as Ingrid Paulson)
*When Ladies Meet* (Mary "Minnie" Howard)

**1942**

*They All Kissed the Bride* (Margaret J. Drew)
*Reunion in France* (Michèle "Mike" de la Becque)

**1943**

*Above Suspicion* (Frances Myles)

**1944**

*Hollywood Canteen* (as herself)

**1945**

*Mildred Pierce* (Mildred Pierce Beragon)

**1946**

*Humoresque* (Helen Wright)

**1947**

*Possessed* (Louise Howell Graham)
*Daisy Kenyon* (Daisy Kenyon)

**1949**

*Flamingo Road* (Lane Bellamy)

**1950**

*The Damned Don't Cry* (Ethel Whitehead/Lorna Hansen Forbes)
*Harriet Craig* (Harriet Craig)

**1951**

*Goodbye, My Fancy* (Agatha Reed)

**1952**

*This Woman is Dangerous* (Elizabeth "Beth" Austin)
*Sudden Fear* (Myra Hudson)

**1953**

*Torch Song* (Jenny Stewart)

**1954**

*Johnny Guitar* (Vienna)

**1955**

*Female on the Beach* (Lynn Markham)
*Queen Bee* (Eva Phillips)

**1956**

*Autumn Leaves* (Millicent Wetherby)

**1957**

*The Story of Esther Costello* (Margaret Landi)

**1959**

*The Best of Everything* (Amanda Farrow)

**1962**

*What Ever Happened to Baby Jane?* (Blanche Hudson)

**1963**

*The Caretakers* (Lucretia Terry)

**1964**

*Strait-Jacket* (Lucy Harbin)

**1965**

*I Saw What You Did* (Amy Nelson)

**1967**

*The Karate Killers* (Amanda True; Made for U.S. television but released theatrically in Europe)
*Berserk!* (Monica Rivers)

**1970**

*Trog* (Dr. Brockton)

# SOURCE NOTES

## INTRODUCTION

1. Vogel, Michelle, ed. *Joan Crawford, Her Life in Letters*. Louisville, Kentucky: Wasteland Press, 2005.
2. Newquist, Roy. *Conversations with Joan Crawford*. Secaucus, New Jersey: Citadel Press, 1980.
3. Chandler, Charlotte. *Not the Girl Next Door, Joan Crawford, A Personal Biography*. New York: Simon & Schuster, 2008.

## CHAPTER 1

1. [epigraph] Higham, Charles, and Joel Greenberg. *The Celluloid Muse: Hollywood Directors Speak*. London: Angus and Robertson, 1969.
2. LaSalle, Mick. *Complicated Women: Sex and Power in Pre-Code Hollywood*. New York: St. Martin's Press, 2000.
3. Chandler, Charlotte. *Not the Girl Next Door: Joan Crawford, A Personal Biography*. New York: Simon & Schuster, 2008.
4. Walker, Alexander. *Stardom, the Hollywood Phenomenon*. London: Michael Joseph, 1970.
5. Newquist, Roy. *Conversations with Joan Crawford*. Secaucus, New Jersey: Citadel Press, 1980.
6. Crawford, Joan, with Jane Kesner Ardmore. *A Portrait of Joan*. New York: Doubleday, 1962.
7. Robinson, David. *Hollywood in the Twenties*. New York: A.S. Barnes & Co./London: The Tantivy Press, 1968.

8. LaSalle (op. cit.).
9. Dumont, Hervé. *Frank Borzage*. Jefferson, North Carolina: McFarland & Co., 2006.
10. Quoted in Thomas, Bob. *Thalberg, Life and Legend*. New York: Doubleday, 1969.
11. Crawford, Joan, with Jane Kesner Ardmore (op. cit.).
12. Ibid.
13. Ibid.
14. Bret, David. *Joan Crawford, Hollywood Martyr*. London: Robson Books, 2006.
15. Crawford, Joan, with Jane Kesner Ardmore (op. cit.).
16. Kobal, John. *People Will Talk. Personal Conversations with the Legends of Hollywood*. London: Aurum Press, 1986.
17. Thomas, Bob. *Joan Crawford, a Biography*. New York: Simon & Schuster, 1978.
18. Shipman, David. *The Great Movie Stars: The Golden Years*. London: Hamlyn, 1970.
19. Chandler, Charlotte (op. cit.).
20. Crawford, Joan, with Jane Kesner Ardmore (op. cit.).
21. Newquist, Roy (op. cit.).
22. LaSalle, Mick (op. cit.).
23. Thomas, Bob. *Thalberg* (op. cit.).
24. Vogel, Michelle, ed. *Joan Crawford: Her Life in Letters*. Louisville, Kentucky: Wasteland Press, 2005.

## CHAPTER 2

1. [epigraph] Newquist, Roy. *Conversations with Joan Crawford.* Secaucus, New Jersey: Citadel Press, 1980.
2. Thomas, Bob. *Joan Crawford, a Biography.* New York: Simon & Schuster, 1978.
3. Ardmore, J. C. *A Portrait of Joan.* New York: Doubleday, 1962.
4. Newquist, Roy. (op. cit).
5. Gutner, Howard. *Gowns by Adrian: The MGM Years 1928–1941.* New York: Harry N. Abrams Inc., 2001.
6. *Vogue,* February 1, 1938.
7. Gutner (op. cit).
8. Ibid.
9. Ibid.
10. Webb, Michael. *Hollywood: Legend and Reality.* Boston/ Washington D.C.: Little, Brown & Co./Smithsonian Institution, 1986.
11. Sharaff, Irene. *Broadway and Hollywood: Costumes by Irene Sharaff.* New York: Van Nostrand, Reinhold, 1976.
12. Chandler, Charlotte. *Not the Girl Next Door: Joan Crawford, A Personal Biography.* New York: Simon & Schuster, 2008.
13. Ibid.
14. Vieira, Mark A. *Hurrell's Hollywood Portraits.* New York: Harry N. Abrams Inc., 1997.
15. Ibid.
16. Kobal, John. *Legends: Joan Crawford.* London: Pavilion Books, 1986.
17. Vieira (op. cit.).
18. Ibid.
19. Kobal, John. *People Will Talk: Personal Conversations with the Legends of Hollywood.* London: Aurum Press, 1986.
20. Ibid.
21. Vieira (op. cit.).
22. Thomas (op. cit.).
23. Ardmore (op. cit.).
24. LaSalle, Mick, e-mail to author.
25. Newquist (op. cit.).
26. Bret, David. *Joan Crawford: Hollywood Martyr.* London: Robson Books, 2005.
27. Newquist (op. cit.).
28. Ibid.
29. Ardmore (op. cit.).
30. Bret (op. cit.).
31. LaSalle, Mick. *Complicated Women: Sex and Power in Pre-Code Hollywood.* New York: St. Martin's Press, 2000.
32. Shipman, David. *The Great Movie Stars: The Golden Years.* London: Hamlyn, 1970.
33. Vogel, Michelle, ed. *Joan Crawford: Her Life in Letters.* Louisville, Kentucky: Wasteland Press, 2005.
34. Walker, Alexander. *Stardom: The Hollywood Phenomenon.* London: Michael Joseph, 1970.
35. Kobal. *People Will Talk* (op. cit.).
36. Ardmore (op. cit.).
37. LaSalle. *Complicated Women* (op. cit.).
38. Ardmore (op. cit.).
39. Ibid.
40. Walker (op.cit.).
41. Gutner (op. cit.).
42. Walker (op. cit.).
43. Ardmore (op. cit.).
44. Kleiner, Dick, with Jackie Cooper. *Please Don't Shoot My Dog: The Autobiography of Jackie Cooper.* New York: Morrow, 1981.
45. Kobal. *People Will Talk* (op. cit.).
46. Newquist (op. cit.).
47. LoBianco, Lorraine. Turner Classic Movies website, http://www.tcmdb.com/title/title.jsp?stid=1184&atid=7233&category=Articles&titleName=Today%20We%20Live&menuName=MAIN
48. Hillier, Jim, and Peter Wollen, editors. *Howard Hawks, American Artist.* London: BFI Publishing, 1996.
49. Bret (op. cit.).
50. Ardmore (op. cit.).
51. Gutner (op. cit.).
52. Newquist (op. cit.).
53. Bret (op. cit.).
54. Kobal, *People Will Talk* (op. cit.).
55. Thomas (op. cit.).
56. Gutner (op. cit.).
57. Ardmore (op. cit.).
58. Ibid.
59. Ibid.
60. Ibid.
61. *Films in Review,* December 1956.

## CHAPTER 3

1. [epigraph] Ross, Lillian and Helen Ross. *The Player.* New York: Simon & Schuster, 1962.
2. Walker (op. cit.).
3. Newquist (op. cit.).
4. Ibid.
5. Ibid.
6. Gutner (op. cit.).
7. Bret (op. cit.).
8. Vogel (op. cit.).
9. Newquist (op. cit.).
10. Ibid.
11. Dumont, Hervé. *Frank Borzage: The Life and Films of a Hollywood Romantic.* Jefferson, North Carolina: McFarland & Co., 2006.
12. Viviani, Christian. *Dictionnaire du Cinéma.* Paris: Larousse, 1986.
13. Newquist (op. cit.).
14. Clarens, Carlos. *Cukor.* London: Secker and Warburg, 1976.
15. Newquist (op. cit.).
16. Ardmore (op. cit.).
17. Newquist (op. cit.).
18. Dumont (op. cit.).
19. Geist, Kenneth L. *Pictures Will Talk: The Life and Films of Joseph L. Mankiewicz.* New York: Charles Scribner's Sons, 1978.
20. Thomas (op. cit.).

21. Kobal, John. *People Will Talk.* (op. cit.).

22. Bret (op. cit.).

23. Vogel (op. cit.).

## CHAPTER 4

1. [epigraph] Haskell, Molly. *From Reverence to Rape.* New York: Holt, Rinehart and Winston, 1974.

2. Newquist (op. cit.).

3. Ibid.

4. Higham, Charles, and Joel Greenberg. *The Celluloid Muse: Hollywood Directors Speak.* London: Angus and Robertson, 1969.

5. Ardmore (op. cit.).

6. Friedrich, Otto. *City of Nets.* London: Headline Publishing, 1986.

7. Quoted in Greene, Graham. *Garbo and the Night Watchmen.* London: Secker and Warburg, 1971.

8. Bret (op. cit.).

9. Thomas (op. cit.).

10. Bret (op. cit.).

11. Kobal. *People Will Talk* (op. cit.).

12. Thomas (op. cit.).

13. Bret (op. cit.).

14. Newquist (op. cit.).

15. Ibid.

16. Ardmore (op. cit.).

17. Thomas (op. cit.).

18. Walker. *Stardom: The Hollywood Phenomenon* (op. cit.).

19. Thomas (op. cit.).

20. Ardmore (op. cit.).

21. Thomas (op. cit.).

22. Bret (op. cit.).

23. Thomas (op. cit.).

24. Higham, Charles and Joel Greenberg. *Hollywood in the Forties.* New York: A. S. Barnes & Co./London: The Tantivy Press, 1968.

25. Walker (op. cit.).

26. Ardmore (op. cit.).

27. Thomas (op. cit.).

28. Ibid.

29. Agee, James. *Film Writing and Selected Journalism.* New York: Library of America, 2005.

30. Thomas (op. cit).

31. Newquist (op. cit.).

32. Walker (op. cit.).

33. Vogel (op. cit.).

34. Ibid.

35. Douglas, Kirk. *The Ragman's Son.* New York: Simon & Schuster, 1988.

36. Ardmore (op. cit.).

37. Thomas (op. cit.).

38. Ibid.

39. Scorsese, Martin introducing *Johnny Guitar* on British-released DVD (Universal, DVD, 823 401 1.11).

40. Thomas (op. cit.).

41. Newquist (op. cit.).

42. Thomas (op. cit.).

43. Ibid.

44. Ardmore (op. cit.).

45. Interview with John Deighton. *Today's Cinema*, September 1969.

46. Higham and Greenberg. *The Celluloid Muse.*

47. Ardmore (op. cit.).

48. Thomas (op. cit.).

49. Newquist (op. cit.).

50. Higham and Greenberg. *The Celluloid Muse.*

51. *The New York Times*, May 22, 1977.